Let's Explore
Diabetes with Owls

Let's Explore Diabetes with Owls

David Sedaris

BACK BAY BOOKS
Little, Brown and Company
New York   Boston   London

Back Bay Books / Little, Brown and Company
Hachette Book Group
237 Park Avenue, New York, NY 10017
littlebrown.com

The publisher is not responsible for websites (or their content) that are not owned by the publisher.

Acknowledgment is made to the following, in which the stories in this collection first appeared, some differently titled or in slightly different form: *The New Yorker*: "Laugh, Kookaburra," "Dentists Without Borders," "A Guy Walks into a Bar Car," "Author, Author," "Memory Laps," "Easy, Tiger," "A Cold Case," "Loggerheads," "Standing By," "Understanding Understanding Owls"; *The Guardian*: "#2 to Go"; *Times of London Sunday Magazine*: "Rubbish"; *Prospect*: "If I Ruled the World"; *GQ*: "Just a Quick E-mail"; *Esquire*: "Dog Days"; *The Best American Essays 2010* and *The Best American Travel Writing 2010*: "A Guy Walks into a Bar Car."

Printed in the United States of America

Originally published in hardcover by Little, Brown and Company, April 2013
First Back Bay / Little, Brown and Company international mass market edition, April 2014

10 9 8 7 6 5 4 3 2 1

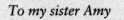

To my sister Amy

Contents

Author's Note

Over the years I've met quite a few teenagers who participate in what is called "Forensics." It's basically a cross between speech and debate. Students take published short stories and essays, edit them down to a predetermined length, and recite them competitively. To that end, as part of the "Etc." in this book's subtitle, I have written six brief monologues that young people might deliver before a panel of judges. I believe these stories should be self-evident. They're the pieces in which I am a woman, a father, and a sixteen-year-old girl with a fake British accent.

Let's Explore
Diabetes with Owls

Dentists Without Borders

One thing that puzzled me during the American health-care debate was all the talk about socialized medicine and how ineffective it's supposed to be. The Canadian plan was likened to genocide, but even worse were the ones in Europe, where patients languished on filthy cots, waiting for aspirin to be invented. I don't know where these people get their ideas, but my experiences in France, where I've lived off and on for the past thirteen years, have all been good. A house call in Paris will run you around fifty dollars. I was tempted to arrange one the last time I had a kidney stone, but waiting even ten minutes seemed out of the question, so instead I took the subway to the nearest hospital. In the center of town, where we're lucky enough to have an apartment, most of my needs are within arm's reach. There's a pharmacy right around the corner, and two blocks farther is the office of my physician, Dr. Médioni.

Twice I've called on a Saturday morning, and, after answering the phone himself, he has told me to come on over. These visits too cost around fifty dollars. The last time I went, I had a red thunderbolt bisecting my left eyeball.

The doctor looked at it for a moment, and then took a seat behind his desk. "I wouldn't worry about it if I were you," he said. "A thing like that, it should be gone in a day or two."

"Well, where did it come from?" I asked. "How did I get it?"

"How do we get most things?" he answered.

"We buy them?"

The time before that, I was lying in bed and found a lump on my right side, just below my rib cage. It was like a deviled egg tucked beneath my skin. *Cancer,* I thought. A phone call and twenty minutes later, I was stretched out on the examining table with my shirt raised.

"Oh, that's nothing," the doctor said. "A little fatty tumor. Dogs get them all the time."

I thought of other things dogs have that I don't want: Dewclaws, for example. Hookworms. "Can I have it removed?"

"I guess you could, but why would you want to?"

He made me feel vain and frivolous for even thinking about it. "You're right," I told him. "I'll just pull my bathing suit up a little higher."

When I asked if the tumor would get any bigger, the doctor gave it a gentle squeeze. "Bigger? Sure, probably."

"Will it get a *lot* bigger?"

"No."

"Why not?" I asked.

And he said, sounding suddenly weary, "I don't know. Why don't trees touch the sky?"

Médioni works from an apartment on the third floor of a handsome nineteenth-century building, and, on leaving, I always think, *Wait a minute. Did I see a diploma on his wall? Could "Doctor" possibly be the man's first name?* He's not indifferent. It's just that I expect a little something more than "It'll go away." The thunderbolt cleared up, just as he said it would, and I've since met dozens of people who have fatty tumors and get along just fine. Maybe, being American, I want bigger names for things. I also expect a bit more gravity. "I've run some tests," I'd like to hear, "and discovered that what you have is called a bilateral ganglial abasement, or, in layman's terms, a cartoidal rupture of the venal septrumus. Dogs get these all the time, and most often they die. That's why I'd like us to proceed with the utmost caution."

For my fifty dollars, I want to leave the doctor's office in tears, but instead I walk out feeling like a hypochondriac, which is one of the few things I'm actually not. If my French physician is a little disappointing, my French periodontist more than makes up for it. I have nothing but good things to say about Dr. Guig, who, gumwise, has really brought me back from the abyss. Twice in the course of our decadelong relationship, he's performed surgical interventions. Then, last year, he removed four of my lower incisors, drilled down into my jawbone, and cemented in place two posts. First, though, he sat me down and explained the procedure, using lots of big words that allowed me to feel tragic and important. "I'm going to perform the surgery at nine o'clock on Tuesday morning, and it should take, at most, three hours," he said—all of this, as usual, in French. "At six that evening, you'll go to the dentist for your temporary implants, but still I'd like you to block out that entire day."

I asked my boyfriend, Hugh, when I got home, "Where did he think I was going to go with four missing teeth?"

I see Dr. Guig for surgery and consultations, but the regular, twice-a-year deep cleanings are performed by his associate, a woman named Dr. Barras. What she does in my mouth is unspeakable, and because it causes me to sweat, I've taken to bringing a second set of clothes and changing in the bathroom before I leave for home. "Oh, Monsieur Sedaris," she chuckles. "You are such a child."

A year ago, I arrived and announced that, since my previous visit, I'd been flossing every night. I thought this might elicit some praise—"How dedicated you are, how disciplined!"—but instead she said, "Oh, there's no need."

It was the same when I complained about all the gaps between my teeth. "I had braces when I was young, but maybe I need them again," I told her. An American dentist would have referred me to an orthodontist, but, to Dr. Barras, I was just being hysterical. "You have what we in France call 'good time teeth,'" she said. "Why on earth would you want to change them?"

"Um, because I can floss with the sash to my bathrobe?"

"Hey," she said, "enough with the flossing. You have better ways to spend your evenings."

I guess that's where the good times come in.

Dr. Barras has a sick mother and a long-haired cat named Andy. As I lie there sweating with my trap wide open, she runs her electric hook under my gum line, and catches me up on her life since my last visit. I always leave with a mouthful of blood, yet I always look forward to my next appointment. She and Dr. Guig are *my* people, completely independent of Hugh, and though it's a stretch to label them friends, I think they'd miss me if I died of a fatty tumor.

Something similar is happening with my dentist, Dr. Granat. He didn't fabricate my implants—that was the work of a prosthodontist—but he took the molds and made certain that the teeth fit. This was done during five visits in the winter of 2011. Once a week, I'd show up at the office and climb into his reclining chair. Then I'd sink back with my mouth open. "*Ça va?*" he'd ask every five minutes or so, meaning, "All right?" And I'd release a little tone. Like a doorbell. "*E-um.*"

Implants come in two stages. The first teeth that get screwed in, the temporaries, are blocky, and the color is off. The second ones are more refined and are somehow dyed or painted to match their neighbors. My four false incisors are connected to form a single unit and were secured into place with an actual screwdriver. Because the teeth affect one's bite, the positioning has to be exact, so my dentist would put them in and then remove them to make minor adjustments. Put them in, take them out. Over and over. All the pain was behind me by this point, so I just lay there, trying to be a good patient.

Dr. Granat keeps a small muted television mounted near the ceiling, and each time I come it is tuned to the French travel channel—Voyage, it's called. Once, I watched a group of mountain people decorate a yak. They didn't string lights on it, but everything else seemed fair game: ribbons, bells, silver sheaths for the tips of its horns.

"Ça va?"

"E-um."

Another week we were somewhere in Africa, where a family of five dug into the ground and unearthed what looked to be a burrow full of mice. Dr. Granat's assistant came into the room to ask a question, and when I looked back at the screen the mice had been skinned and placed, kebab-like, on sharp sticks. Then came another distraction, and when I looked up again the family in Africa were grilling the mice over a campfire, and eating them with their fingers.

"Ça va?" Dr. Granat asked, and I raised my hand, international dental sign language for "There is something vital I need to communicate." He removed his screwdriver from my mouth, and I pointed to the screen. "Ils ont mangé des souris en brochette," I told him, meaning, "They have eaten some mice on skewers."

He looked up at the little TV. "Ah, oui?"

A regular viewer of the travel channel, Dr. Granat is surprised by nothing. He's seen it all and is quite the traveler himself. As is Dr. Guig. Dr. Barras hasn't gone anywhere exciting lately, but what with her mother, how can she? With all these dental professionals in my life, you'd think I'd look less like a jack-o'-lantern. You'd think I could bite into an ear of corn, or at least tear meat from a chicken bone, but that won't happen for another few years, not until we tackle my two front teeth and the wobbly second incisors that flank them. "But after that's done I'll still need to come regularly, won't I?" I said to Dr. Guig, almost panicked. "My gum disease isn't cured, is it?"

I've gone from avoiding dentists and periodontists to practically stalking them, not in some quest for a Hollywood smile but because I enjoy their company. I'm happy in their waiting rooms, the coffee tables heaped with *Gala* and *Madame Figaro*. I like their mumbled French, spoken from behind Tyvek masks. None of them ever call me David, no matter how often I invite them to. Rather, I'm Monsieur Sedaris, not my father but the smaller, Continental model. Monsieur Sedaris with the four lower implants. Monsieur Sedaris with the good-time teeth, sweating so fiercely he leaves the office two kilos lighter. That's me, pointing to the bathroom and asking the receptionist if I may use the sandbox, me traipsing down the stairs in a fresh set of clothes, my smile bittersweet and drearied with blood, counting the days until I can come back and return myself to this curious, socialized care.

Attaboy

It was winter and I was in New York, killing time
before a movie. Week-old snow lay moldering along
the curbs, and I was just noticing all the trash in it
when I heard a man yell, "Citizen's arrest!" I guess
I knew that such a thing existed, but you never hear
of anyone taking advantage of it, so I assumed it was
a joke—a candid-camera type of thing, or maybe a
student making a movie.

"Citizen's arrest!" the man repeated. He was
standing in front of a grocery store called Fairway,
on Broadway and 74th. Neat, pewter-colored hair
covered the back and sides of his head, but the top of
it was bald and raw-looking from the cold. The man
had a puffy down jacket on, and as I moved closer,
I saw that he was touching the shoulder of a teenage
boy, not gripping him so much as tagging him, claim-
ing him.

"Citizen's arrest. Citizen's arrest!" I wondered
what crime had been committed, and, judging from
the people around me, many of whom had stopped

or at least slowed down, I wasn't alone. Something silver had dropped to the ground, and just as I saw that it was a Magic Marker, a couple ran out of the store—the boy's parents, I assumed, for they raced right to his side. "Citizen's arrest," the man repeated. "He was graffitiing the mailbox!"

I expected the parents to say, "He was *what?*" But rather than scolding their guilty-looking son, they turned on the guy who had caught him. "Who gave you the right to touch our child?"

"But the mailbox," the man explained, "I saw him—"

"I don't care what he was doing," the woman said. "You have no right touching my son." She made it sound like a sexual thing, like he'd had his hand up the boy's ass rather than resting, weightless, on his shoulder. "Just who the hell do you think you are?" She turned to her husband. "Douglas, call the police."

"I'm two steps ahead of you," he said.

Watching him dial, I thought, *Really? This is your reaction?* If I were thirteen and I'd been caught graffitiing a mailbox, my parents would have thanked the man and shaken his hand. "We'll take it from here," they'd have assured him. Then, in full view of the crowd, they would have beaten me— not a couple of light stage slaps but the real thing, with loosened teeth and muffled pleas for mercy. And that would have been just the start of it. Not only would my allowance have been cut off, but if I ever wanted freedom again, I'd have had to pay for it: every hour outside my room costing me a dollar, which is like, I don't know, seventeen dollars in today's currency.

"But how do you expect me to work if I can't go outside?" I'd have wept.

"You should have thought about that before you defaced that mailbox," my father would have told me, this while my mother held my arms behind my back and he hit me with a golf club. In the balls.

Never would they have blindly defended me or even asked for my side of the story, as that would have put me on the same level as the adult. If a strange man accused you of doing something illegal, you did it. Or you might as well have done it. Or you were at least thinking about doing it. There was no negotiating, no "parenting" the way there is now. All these young mothers chauffeuring their volcanic three-year-olds through the grocery store. The child's name always sounds vaguely presidential, and he or she tends to act accordingly. "Mommy hears what you're saying about treats," the woman will say, "but right now she needs you to let go of her hair and put the chocolate-covered Life Savers back where they came from."

"No!" screams McKinley or Madison, Kennedy or Lincoln or beet-faced baby Reagan. Looking on, I always want to intervene. "Listen," I'd like to say, "I'm not a parent myself, but I think the best solution at this point is to slap that child across the face. It won't stop its crying, but at least now it'll be doing it for a good reason."

I don't know how these couples do it, spend hours each night tucking their kids in, reading them books about misguided kittens or seals who wear uniforms, and then *re*reading them if the child so orders. In my house, our parents put us to bed with two simple words: "Shut up." That was always the last thing we heard before our lights were turned off. Our artwork did not hang on the refrigerator or anywhere near it, because our parents recognized it for what it was: crap. They did not live in a child's house, we lived in theirs.

Neither were we allowed to choose what we ate. I have a friend whose seven-year-old will only consider something if it's white. Had I tried that, my parents would have said, "You're on," and served me a bowl of paste, followed by joint compound, and, maybe if I was good, some semen. They weren't considered strict by any means. They weren't abusive. The rules were just different back then, especially in regard to corporal punishment. Not only could you hit your own children, but you could also hit other people's. I was in the fifth grade when someone on our street called my mother a bitch. "I wasn't doing anything out of the ordinary," she said to my father. "Just driving Lisa home from her doctor's appointment, and out of nowhere this boy yelled it out." Four months pregnant with my brother, Paul, she lit a cigarette and poured herself some wine from the fifty-gallon jug beside the toaster.

"What boy?" my father asked. He had just returned from work and was standing in the kitchen, drinking a glass of gin with some ice in it. Before him on the counter were crackers and a rectangle of cream cheese smothered in golden sauce. "Oh no, you don't," he said as I reached for the knife. "This is for me, goddamnit."

"But can't I just—"

"You want an after-work snack, get a job," he said, forgetting, I guess, that I was eleven.

"So who's this kid who called your mother a bitch?" he asked. "Give me his name so I can go talk to him."

I said I didn't know, and he looked at me with disappointment, the way you might at anyone who was woefully unconnected. "Well, can't you at least guess?"

"Beats me." No one on our street had reason to hate my mother. It was likely someone just road testing his new curse word—a little late too, as our end of the block had discovered it months earlier. "It means 'female dog,'" I'd explained to my sisters, "but it also means 'a woman who's crabby and won't let you be yourself.'"

The day that someone called my mother a bitch was not remarkable. My father returned from work, like always. He had his drink and his fancy snack. When my mother announced dinner, he took off his jacket, stepped out of his trousers, and took his seat alongside the rest of us. From the tabletop up, he was all business casual—the ironed shirt, the loosened tie—but from there on down it was just briefs and bare legs. "So I understand from your mother that someone called her a not very nice word this afternoon," he said, turning to my older sister. "You were in the car with her. Any idea who it was?"

Lisa speculated that it was Tommy Reimer, not

because she got a clear look at him but because it happened near his house.

"Tommy Reimer, huh?" My father looked across the table to my mother. "Isn't that one of Arthur's boys?"

"Oh, Lou, let it go," my mother said.

"What do you mean, let it go? A kid who uses language like that has got a problem, and I'm going to see that it gets fixed."

"Maybe I misunderstood him," my mother said. "Or maybe he thought I was someone else. That's it, most likely."

"I'll be sure to clear that up when I talk to him," my father said, his cue that the subject was closed and that now we would move on to something else. When her children were grown and gone from the house, my mother would eat late, often by herself in front of the TV, hours after she had served our father, but back then, like most every other family on our street, we had dinner at six. On this particular night the sun was still out. It was early September, and though I don't remember what we were eating, I can clearly recall cringing at the sound of the doorbell.

Oh God, I thought, as did everyone else at the table. For when it was dinnertime and someone came calling, it was always our father who insisted on answering the door and on telling whoever it was, very firmly, that it was not a good idea to interrupt people while they were eating. It could be a woman from down the street or maybe one of our friends. It might be a Girl Scout selling cookies or a strange man with a petition, but when that door was flung open, everyone on the other side of it wore the same expression, a startled, quizzical look that translated, in that gentler, more polite time, to "Where are your pants, sir?"

Lisa had left school early that day. A classmate was supposed to drop off a homework assignment, and worried that it might be her, she jumped up and ran into the other room, calling, "That's okay, I've got it."

My father raised himself and then sat back down. "You tell whoever it is that we're eating our supper, damn it." He scowled at my mother. "Who the hell drops by at this hour?"

We all strained to hear who our visitor was, and when Lisa said, "Oh, hi, Tommy," our father leapt up and ran to the door. By the time we got there, the boy, who was one grade behind me, was pinned against the redwood siding of our carport. My father had him by the neck, raised off the ground, and his little legs were flailing.

"Dad," we called. "Dad, stop. That's the wrong boy. You're looking for Tommy Reimer, but this is Tommy Williams!"

"It's who?" In his work shirt and underpants, he looked powerful but also cartoonish, like a bear dressed up for a job interview.

"Lou, for God's sake, put that boy down," our mother said.

My father lowered Tommy to the ground, where he doubled over and gasped for breath. He was a chubby kid, and his face, which was freckled and normally pale, was now the color of a valentine.

"Hey, son," my father said, so sweet suddenly, so transparent. He put his hand on Tommy's shoulder. "You all right? Want some ice cream? How about some ice cream?"

"That's okay," Tommy croaked. "I think I'll just go home."

"Actually, no," my father said, and he guided the boy through our open door. "We'd like you to stay for a while. Come on inside and join us." He turned to me and lowered his voice. "Find some ice cream, damn it."

If there'd been anything decent in the house, anything approaching *real* ice cream, it would have been eaten long ago. I knew this, so I bypassed the freezer in the kitchen and the secondary freezer in the toolshed and went to the neglected, tundralike one in the basement. Behind the chickens bought years earlier on sale, and the roasts encased like chestnuts in blood-tinted frost, I found a tub of ice milk, vanilla-flavored, and the color of pus. It had been frozen for so long that even I, a child, was made to feel old by the price tag. "Thirty-five cents! You can't get naught for that nowadays."

That this was my thought while my friend sat, red-throated as a bullfinch, at our dining room table speaks volumes about that era. Even if Tommy had escaped captivity and run back home, it's not likely his parents would have called the police, much less sued and sent us to the poorhouse. No angry words would be exchanged the next time his father passed mine in the street, and why would there be? Their son hadn't died, just gone without oxygen for a minute. And might that not make him stronger?

On opening the ice milk I saw that it had thawed before its last freezing. Beneath an inch of what looked like snow, the texture was wrong, too slick-looking and so hard it bent the spoon and came out in slender, translucent chips. It took everything I had to chisel out a bowlful of them, but in time I did. Then I carried it in to Tommy and set it before him on the table. It was strange, him faced with dessert while the rest of us were still working on dinner. For a minute he just sat there, staring down and blinking. My father chose to interpret this as an expression of wonder. "That's right," he said. "It's all for you. I'm sure we can even find some more if you want it."

Tommy looked at us, seven sets of eyes, watching, and he reached for his spoon.

"There you go," my father said. "Attaboy. Eat up."

Think Differenter

Of the many expressions we Americans tend to overuse, I think the most irritating is "Blind people are human too." They are, I guess, but saying so makes you sound preachy and involved, like all your best friends are blind—which they're probably not. I, personally, don't know any blind people, though the guy I used to buy my newspapers from had pretty bad cataracts. His left eye had a patch over it, and the right one reminded me of the sky in a werewolf movie, this pale blue moon obscured by drifting clouds. Still, though, he could see well enough to spot a Canadian quarter. "Oh no you don't," he said to me the last time I bought something. Then he actually grabbed my hand!

I pulled it back. "Well, excuussse me." Then I said, "I think it's a-boat time I take my business elsewhere." Normally I say "about," but I wanted him to think I was Canadian, which could have been true if I was born a couple hundred miles to the north.

The son of a bitch half-blind person. I'm through defending the likes of him.

Number two on my irritating expression list is "I'll never forget the time..." People say this to me, and I think, *Yawn. Am I ever in for a boring story.* Take this Fourth of July party, the one thrown every year at the apartment complex I live at. I went last summer, and it was me, this guy Teddy from two doors down, and a woman from the ground floor all standing around the pool. The fireworks had ended, and all of a sudden, out of nowhere, Teddy looks down into the water. "I'll never forget the time my five-year-old daughter drowned," he told us, all mournful, as if it happened that week and not an entire year ago.

The woman from the ground floor put her hand on his shoulder. "Oh my God," she said. "That is the saddest thing I ever heard in my life."

I, meanwhile, was standing there thinking that you should never say never, especially in regard to what you'll remember. People get older, and you'd be surprised by what they forget. Like, for example, a few weeks back I called my mother to wish her a happy birthday, her eightieth. "I bet you wish that Dad was still alive," I said. "That way the two of you could celebrate together."

"But he *is* still alive," she told me.

"He is?"

"Well, of course," she said. "Who do you think answered the phone?"

Here I am, just turned fifty, and I forgot that my father isn't dead yet! In my defense, though, he's pretty close to it. Healthy enough for the moment, but he doesn't do any of the stuff he used to do, like give me money or teach me to ride bikes.

There are things you forget naturally—computer passwords, your father's continuing relationship with life—and then there are things you can't forget but wish you could. Once, for instance, when I was in the third grade, I saw our dog Pepper chew the head off a baby rabbit. I mean right off too, the way I'd pop the lid from an aspirin bottle. That, I can recall just like it was yesterday, while my first child being born—total blank. I know I was in the delivery room. I even remember what I was listening to on my Walkman, but as for the actual kid coming out— nothing. I can't even tell you if it was a boy or a girl, but that's natural for a first marriage.

The Walkman, though, I'll never forget its weight and the way it fit into my jacket pocket. Now, of course, it would be like carrying around a brick, but at the time it was hard to imagine anything more modern. When the first iPod came out, I recall think- ing that it would never last. Isn't that funny? It's what old kooks thought when the car was invented, only now the kook was me! I held on to my Walk- man until the iPod shuffle was introduced, at which point I caved in and bought one.

I got remarried as well, but it only lasted until the iPod nano, which the child from that marriage— a boy, I'm pretty sure—threw into the toilet along with my wallet and my car keys. Instead of fishing it all out and getting my hands dirty, I left that wife and kid and moved to where I live now, the apartment complex I mentioned earlier. I thought of replacing my nano, but instead I waited awhile and got an iPhone, which I specifically use not to call either of my ex-wives or the children they tricked me into having. It's a strain on the eyes, but I also read the paper on it, so take that, newsagent—I'm the half-blind one now, and you're out of a job!

The iPhone 2 led to the 3, but I didn't get the 4 or 5 because I'm holding out for the 7, which, I've heard on good authority, can also be used as a Taser. This will mean I'll have just one less thing to carry around. And isn't that technology's job? To lighten our burden? To broaden our horizons? To make it possible to talk to your attorney and listen to a Styx album and check the obituaries in the town where your parents continue to live and videotape a race riot and send a text message and stun someone into submission all at the same time?

Doing it all while driving is illegal where I live, so I'm moving to a place where freedom still means something. I'm not telling you where it is, because I want it to remain unspoiled. I'll just say it's one of the few states left where the mentally ill can legally own firearms. They used to be limited to muskets, but now they can carry or conceal everything a normal person can. If you don't think a mental patient has the right to bring a sawed-off shotgun to the church where his ex-girlfriend is getting married, you're part of the problem. The truth is that crazy people—who are really just regular people but more misunderstood—have as much of a right to protect themselves as we do.

Live with liberty, and your imagination can soar. If I had been born in the state I'm moving to, there's no telling who I might be by now—an oral surgeon, maybe, or perhaps the ruler of the whole U.S. countryside. Other kings would pay me tribute with livestock and precious gems, but deep inside I don't think I'd be any different from who I am today: just a guy with a phone, waiting for the day when he can buy an even better one.

Memory Laps

I always told myself that when I hit fifty I was going to discover opera, not just casually but full force: studying the composers, learning Italian, maybe even buying a cape. It seemed like something an older person could really sink his teeth into—that's why I put it off for so long. Then I turned fifty, and, instead of opera, I discovered swimming. Or, rather, I *rediscovered* swimming. I've known how to do it since I was ten and took lessons at the Raleigh Country Club. There was a better place, the Carolina Country Club, but I don't believe they admitted Yankees. Jews either, if my memory serves me correctly. The only blacks I recall were employees, and they were known to everyone, even children, by their first names. The man behind the bar was Ike. You were eleven-year-old Mr. Sedaris.

The better country club operated on the principle that Raleigh mattered, that its old families were fine ones, and that they needed a place where they could enjoy one another's company without being pawed at. Had we not found this laughable, our country club might have felt desperate. Instead, its attitude was *Look at how much money you saved by not being good enough!*

I can't speak for the two clubs' golf courses, but their pools were the same size, and on a hot, windless afternoon you could probably smell them from an equal distance. Chlorine pits is what they were. Chemical baths. In the deep end, my sisters and I would dive for nickels. Toss one in, and by the time we reached it, half of Jefferson's face would be eaten away. Come lunchtime, we'd line up at the snack bar, our hair the texture of cotton candy, our small, burning eyes like little cranberries.

My lessons were taken in June 1966, the first year of our membership. By the following summer, I was on the swim team. This sounds like an accomplishment, but I believe that in 1967 anyone could be on the Raleigh Country Club team. All you had to do was show up and wear an orange Speedo.

Before my first practice, I put swimming in the same category as walking and riding a bike: things one did to get from place to place. I never thought of how well I was doing them. It was only in competing that an activity became fraught and self-conscious. More accurately, it was only in competing with boys. I was fine against girls, especially if they were younger than me. Younger than me and physically challenged was even better. Give me a female opponent with a first-grade education and a leg brace, and I would churn that water like a speedboat. When it came to winning, I never split hairs.

Most of my ribbons were for good sportsmanship, a backhanded compliment if ever there was one. As the starting gun was raised, I would look at my competitors twitching at their places. Parents would shout their boozy encouragement from the sidelines, and it would occur to me that one of us would have to lose, that I could do that for these people. For whether I placed or came in last, all I ultimately felt was relief. The race was over, and now I could go home. Then the next meet would be announced, and it would start again: the sleepless nights, the stomachaches, a crippling and all-encompassing sense of doom. My sisters Lisa and Gretchen were on the team as well, but I don't think it bothered them as much. For me, every meet day was the same. "Mom"—this said with a groan, like someone calling out from beneath a boulder—"I don't feel too good. Maybe we should—"

"Oh no, you don't."

If I had been trying to get out of school, she'd have at least allowed me to plead my case, but then she had no presence at school. At the club she was front and center, laughing it up with Ike at the bar and with the girls in the restaurant beside the putting green. Once summer got going, we'd spend all day at the pool, us swimming and her broasting on one of the deck chairs. Every so often, she'd go into the water to cool off, but she didn't know how to swim and didn't trust us not to drag her under. So she'd sit waist-deep in the kiddie pool, dropping her cigarette ash onto the wet pavement and dissolving it with her finger.

There was a good-size group of women like her, and they were united in their desire to be left alone. Run to your mother with a complaint, and before she could speak one of the others would say, "Oh, come on now. Let's not be a tattletale," or, "You would have lost that tooth anyway. Now get back into the water." I think of them in that terrible heat, no umbrellas, just sunglasses and bottles of tanning oil that left them smelling like coconuts.

The pool was a land of women and children until swim meets, which usually started at six. Then drinks would be ordered and the dads would arrive. For most of the fathers, this was just one more thing they had to turn up for. Their son was likely on his school's football or basketball team. Maybe he played baseball as well. For my dad, though, this was it, and the way I saw it he should have been grateful. Look at all the time my fear of sports was affording him—weekends and evenings free.

In retrospect, I was never an awful swimmer, just average. I'd come in third sometimes, and once or twice, if I was part of a relay team, we'd place first, though I could hardly take credit. Occasionally, we'd have intraclub races, us against us, and in those, as in the larger meets, the star was a boy named Greg Sakas, who was my size but a few years younger, with pale yellow hair and legs no thicker than jumper cables. "God, that Greg Sakas, did you see him go?" my father said on the way home from my first meet. "Man alive, that kid is *faaaantastic*."

In the beginning, it didn't bother me. Greg wasn't stuck-up. His father was decent enough, and everyone adored his mother. She was one of the few moms who could get away with wearing a bikini, a chocolate-colored one that, as the summer advanced, made it look as if she were naked. "That son of yours is really something," I heard my father say to her after the second meet. "You ought to bring a movie camera out here and film him."

On the way home, he repeated the conversation to my mother. "I said to her, 'Send the footage to a professional swimming coach, and he'll be champing at the bit! Your boy is the real thing. Olympic material, I'm telling you. He's got speed, personality, the whole package.'"

Okay, I thought. *You can shut up about Greg Sakas now.*

We had a station wagon at the time, and my sister Gretchen and I were in what we called the "way back"—the spot where groceries usually went. When she was a baby, a dog bit her face and left her with a scar that was almost invisible until she got a tan. Then it looked like someone had chalked the number 1 four times on her cheek and put a strike mark through them.

"It's the kids swimming *against* him I feel sorry for," my father continued. "Those clowns didn't stand a chance. And did you hear what he said when they handed him his blue ribbon? Who the hell knew Greg Sakas could be so funny? Good-looking too. Just an all-around four-star individual."

When she was young, my sister was what we called chunky, and the longer my dad carried on about Greg the better it seemed to draw attention to it. "Hey," I called. "Gretchen's in a sunbeam. Does anybody else smell bacon frying?"

My sister looked at me like, *Weren't we friends just two minutes ago? Where is this coming from?*

"Maybe Mom should put her on a diet," I said. "That way she won't be so fat."

"Actually, that's not a bad idea," my father said.

My mother, newly pregnant and feeling somewhat chunky herself, put her two cents in, and I settled back, triumphant. This was the advantage of having a large family. You didn't want to focus attention on Lisa—Miss Perfect—but there were three, and later four, others to go after, all younger and all with their particular faults: buckteeth, failing grades. It was like shooting fish in a barrel. Even if I wound up getting punished, it was still a way of changing the channel, switching in this case from *The Greg Show* to *The David Show,* which was today sponsored by Gretchen's weight problem. Meanwhile, my sisters had their own channels to change, and when it got to be too much, when our parents could no longer take it, they'd open the car door and throw us out. The spot they favored—had actually blackened with their tire treads—was at the bottom of a steep hill. The distance home wasn't all that great, a half mile, maybe, but it seemed twice as long when it was hot or raining, or, worse yet, during a thunderstorm. "Aw, it's just heat lightning," our father would say. "That's not going to kill anybody. Now get the hell out of my car."

Neighbors would pass, and when they honked I'd remember that I was in my Speedo. Then I'd wrap

my towel like a skirt around my waist and remind
my sisters that this was not girlish but *Egyptian,*
thank you very much.

Drawing attention to Gretchen's weight was the sort
of behavior my mother referred to as "stirring the
turd," and I did it a lot that summer. *Dad wants
Greg Sakas to be his son instead of me,* I thought,
and in response I made myself the kind of kid that
nobody could like.

"What on earth has gotten into you?" my mother
kept asking.

I wanted to tell her, but more than that I wanted
her to notice it on her own. *How can you not?* I kept
wondering. *It's all he ever talks about.*

The next swim meet was a replay of the first
two. Coming home, I was once again in the "way
·back"—anything to put some distance between me
and my father. "I'll tell you what—that Greg is
magic. Success is written all over his face, and when
it happens I'm going to say, 'Hey, buddy, remember
me? I'm the one who first realized how special you
are.' "

He talked as if he actually knew stuff about swimming, like he was a talent scout for Poseidon or
something. "The butterfly's his strong suit, but let's
not discount his crawl or, hell, even his breaststroke,
for that matter. Seeing that kid in the water is like
seeing a shark!"

His talk was supposedly directed at my mother,
who'd stare out the window and sometimes sigh,

"Oh gosh, Lou. I don't know." She never said anything to keep the conversation going, so I could only believe that he was saying these things for my benefit. Why else would he be speaking so loudly, and catching my eye in the rearview mirror?

One week, while riding home, I took my sister Amy's Barbie doll, tied her feet to the end of my beach towel, and lowered her out the way-back window, dragging her behind us as we drove along. Every so often I'd reel her back in and look at the damage—the way the asphalt had worn the hair off one side of her head, whittled her ski-jump nose down to nothing. *What,* I wondered, *was Greg up to at that exact moment?* Did *his* father like him as much as mine did? He was an only child, so chances were he got the star treatment at home as well as at the club. I lowered the doll back out the window and let go of the towel. The car behind us honked, and I ducked down low and gave the driver the finger.

By mid-July, I was begging to quit the team, but my parents wouldn't allow it. "Oh, you're a good swimmer," my mother said. "Not the best, maybe, but so what? Who wants to be the best at something you do in a bathing suit?"

In the winter, my Greek grandmother was hit by a truck and moved from New York State to live with us. Bringing her to the club would have depressed people. The mournful black dresses, the long gray hair pinned into an Old Country bun, she was the human equivalent of a storm cloud. I thought she'd put a crimp in our upcoming pool schedule, but when Memorial Day arrived, it was business as usual. "She's a big girl," my mother said. "Let her stay home by herself."

"Well, shouldn't we be back by five, just in case she falls down the stairs or something?" I didn't want her to ruin my summer—just to keep me off the swim team. "I could come home and sit with her."

"The hell you will," my mother said. "A nice steep fall is just what I'm hoping for."

I thought the birth of my brother, Paul, might limit our pool hours as well, but, again, no luck. It can't have been healthy for a six-month-old in that hot sun. Maybe that's why he never cried. He was in shock—the only baby I'd ever seen with a tan line. "Cute kid," Greg said one afternoon, and I worried that he might win over Paul and my mother the way he had my father.

The summer of '68 was even worse than the one before it. The club started serving a once-a-week prime-rib dinner, dress up—which meant my blue wool sports coat. Sweating over my fruit cocktail, I'd watch my father make his rounds, stopping at the Sakases' table and laying his hand on Greg's shoulder the way he'd never once put it on mine. There weren't many people I truly hated back then— thirty, maybe forty-five at most—and Greg was at the top of my list. The killer was that it wasn't even my idea. I was being *forced* to hate him, or, rather, forced to hate myself for not being him. It's not as if the two of us were all that different, really: same size, similar build. Greg wasn't exceptional-looking. He was certainly no scholar. I was starting to see that he wasn't all that great a swimmer either. Fast enough, sure, but far too choppy. I brought this to my father's attention, and he attributed my observation to sour grapes: "Maybe you should work on your own stroke before you start criticizing everyone else's."

Things will be better when the summer is over, I kept thinking. We continued going to the club for prime rib, but Greg wasn't always there, and without the swimming there wasn't as much for my dad to carry on about. When fall arrived, he got behind a boy in my Scout troop. But my father didn't really understand what went on in Scouts. The most difficult thing we did that year was wrap potatoes in tinfoil, and I could wrap a potato just as well as the next guy. Then one night while watching *The Andy Williams Show,* he came upon Donny Osmond.

"I just saw this kid on TV, and I mean to tell you, he absolutely knocked my socks off. The singing, the dancing—this boy's going to be huge, you mark my words."

"You didn't discover him," I said the following evening at dinner. "If someone's on *The Andy Williams Show,* it means they were *already* discovered. Stop trying to take credit."

"Well, someone's testy, aren't they?" My father lifted his drink off the table. "I wonder when Donny will be on again."

"It's the Osmond *Brothers,*" I said. "Girls at

school talk about them all the time. It's not a solo act—they're a group."

"Not without him, they're not. Donny's the thunderbolt. Take him out of the picture, and they're nothing."

The next time they were on *The Andy Williams Show*, my father flushed me out of my room and forced me to watch.

"Isn't he fantastic? Just look at that kid! God Almighty, can you believe it?"

Competing against celebrities, people who were not in any sense "real," was a losing game. I knew this as well as I knew my name and troop number, but the more my father carried on about Donny Osmond, the more threatened and insignificant I felt. The thing was that he didn't even like that kind of music. "Well, normally, no," he said, when I brought it up. "Something about Donny, though, makes me like it." He paused. "And the hell of it is he's even younger than you are."

"A year younger."

"Well, that's still younger."

I'd never know if my father did this to hurt me or to spur me on, but on both fronts he was wildly successful. I remember being at the club in the summer of '69, the day that men walked on the moon. Someone put a TV on the lifeguard chair, and we all gathered around, me thinking that at least today something was bigger than Donny Osmond and Greg Sakas, who was actually now a little shorter than I was.

That Labor Day, at the season's final intraclub

meet, I beat Greg in the butterfly. "Were you watching? Did you see that? I won!"

"Maybe you did, but it was only by a hair," my father said on our way home that evening. "Besides, that was, what—one time out of fifty? I don't really see that you've got anything to brag about."

That's when I thought, *Okay, so that's how it is.* My dad was like the Marine Corps, only instead of tearing you to pieces and then putting you back together, he just did the first part and called it a day. Now it seems cruel, abusive even, but this all happened before the invention of self-esteem, which, frankly, I think is a little overrated.

I'm sure my father said plenty of normal things to me when I was growing up, but what stuck, probably because he said it, like, ten thousand times, was "Everything you touch turns to crap." His other catchphrase was "You know what you are? A big fat zero."

I'll show you, I remember thinking. Proving him wrong was what got me out of bed every morning, and when I failed it's what got me back on my feet. I remember calling in the summer of 2008 to tell him my book was number one on the *Times* bestseller list.

"Well, it's not number one on the *Wall Street Journal* list," he said.

"That's not really the list that book people turn to," I told him.

"The hell it isn't," he said. "I turn to it."

"And you're a book person?"

"I read. Sure."

I recalled the copy of *Putt to Win* gathering dust on the backseat of his car. "Of course you read," I said.

Number one on the *Times* list doesn't mean that your book is good—just that a lot of people bought it that week, people who were tricked, maybe, or were never too bright to begin with. It's not like winning the Nobel Prize in Literature, but still, if it's your kid, aren't you supposed to be happy and supportive?

Of course, it complicates things when a lot of that book is about you and what a buffoon you can be. Number one in this particular case meant that a whole lot of people just read about my father sitting around in his underpants and hitting people over the head with spoons. So maybe he had a right to be less than enthusiastic.

When I told him I'd started swimming again, my dad said, "Attaboy." This is the phrase he uses whenever I do something he thinks was his idea.

"I'm going back to college."

"Attaboy."

"I'm thinking of getting my teeth fixed."

"Attaboy."

"On second thought...," I always want to say.

It's not my father's approval that troubles me but my childlike hope that maybe this time it will last. He likes that I've started swimming again, so maybe he'll also like the house I bought ("Boy, they sure saw you coming") or the sports coat I picked up on my last trip to Japan ("You look like a goddamn clown").

Greg Sakas would have got the same treatment eventually, as would any of the other would-be sons my father pitted me against throughout my adolescence. Once they got used to the sweet taste of his approval, he'd have no choice but to snatch it away, not because of anything they did but because it is in his nature. The guy sees a spark and just can't help but stomp it out.

I was in Las Vegas not long ago and looked up to see Donny Osmond smiling down at me from a billboard only slightly smaller than the sky. "*You,*" I whispered.

In the hotel pool a few hours later, I thought of him as I swam my laps. Then I thought of Greg and was carried right back to the Raleigh Country Club. Labor Day, 1969. A big crowd for the intraclub meet, the air smelling of chlorine and smoke from the barbecue pit. The crummy part of swimming is that while you're doing it you can't really see much: the bottom of the pool, certainly, a smudged and fleeting bit of the outside world as you turn your head to breathe. But you can't pick things out—a man's face, for example, watching from the sidelines when, for the first time in your life, you pull ahead and win.

A Friend in the Ghetto

I was in London, squinting out my kitchen window at a distant helicopter, when a sales rep phoned from some overseas call center. "Mr. Sedriz?" he asked. "Is that who I have the pleasure of addressing?" The man spoke with an accent, and though I couldn't exactly place it, I knew that he was poor. His voice had snakes in it. And dysentery, and mangoes.

"I am hoping this morning to interest you in a cell phone," he announced. "But not just *any* cell phone! This one takes pictures that you can send to your friends."

"I'm sorry," I told him. "But I don't have any friends."

He chuckled. "No, but seriously, Mr. Sedriz, this new camera phone is far superior to the one you already have."

When I told him I didn't already have one, he said, "All the better!"

"No," I said, "I don't *want* one. I don't need it."

"How can you not need a cell phone?"

"Because nobody ever calls me?"

"Well, how *can* they?" he argued.

I told him I was fine with my landline.

"But if you have a cell phone, people will look up to you," he said. "I know this for a fact. Also it comes with a free trial period, so maybe you should think of it as a temporary gift!"

Hugh would have hung up the moment his name was mispronounced, but I've never been able to do that, no matter how frustrated I get. There's a short circuit between my brain and my tongue, thus "Leave me the fuck alone" comes out as "Well, maybe. Sure. I guess I can see your point."

This, though, was out of the question. "Listen," I finally said. "You trying to give me a camera phone is like me trying to give you...a raccoon."

There was a pause, and when I realized he didn't know what a raccoon was, I tried substituting it with a similar-sized animal that lived in a poor country. "Or a mongoose," I said. "Or a...honey badger."

"I am going to send you this phone, Mr. Sedriz, and if you're not happy you can return it with no penalty after three weeks."

"But that's just it," I said. "I *won't* be happy. I won't even take it out of the box, and what's the point in receiving something I'll only have to send back?"

The man thought for a moment and sighed. "You, Mr. Sedriz, are down to the earth, and I appreciate that. I can see that you do not want a cell phone, but I did enjoy speaking with you. Do you think I could perhaps call you back one day? We do not have to discuss business but can talk about whatever you like."

"Well, sure," I said. "That would be great."

The following morning my phone rang, and I was genuinely disappointed to find that it wasn't him. The fact was that I'd enjoyed our conversation. The sales part was a little tiresome, but with that behind us, I hoped we could move on to other things, and that listening to him would be like reading the type of book I most enjoy, one about people whose lives are fundamentally different from my own. By this I mean, different in a bad way. Someone who lives in a mansion spun of golden floss, forget it, but someone who lives in an old refrigerator beside a drainage ditch—by all means, call me! Collect, even.

"You need people like that in your life so you can feel better about yourself," my mother used to tell me. The first time she said it, I was fourteen and had recently begun the ninth grade. Our school system had just desegregated, and I wanted to invite one of my new classmates to a party at my grandmother's apartment complex. The girl I had in mind, I'll call her Delicia, was pretty much my exact opposite—black to my white, fat to my thin—and though my family was just middle-class, I felt certain we were wealthy when compared to hers.

The kids who'd been bused to my school were from the south side. This was a part of town we drove through on our way to the beach, always with the car doors locked and the windows rolled up, no matter how hot it was. I wasn't sure which of the run-down houses was Delicia's, but I assumed it was the shackiest. Even dressed up, the girl would have looked like a poor person, not a sassy, defiant one but the kind who had quit struggling and accepted poverty as her lot in life. The clothes she wore seemed secondhand, castoffs suited to a frumpy woman rather than a teenager. Her shoes were crushed down in the back like bedroom slippers, and because of her weight she was frequently out of breath and sweating.

One of the things the north siders learned that year was that black people discriminated against one another just like white people did, and often for the same reasons. Delicia was dark-skinned, and it was that more than her weight that seemed to bring her grief. There was something old-fashioned about her appearance: these full cheeks and round, startled eyes, their whites dazzling in contrast to the rest of her face.

We had two significantly overweight black students at our school that year, and I was always surprised when people confused them for each other. The second girl, Debra, had processed hair, and sticking from it like an ax handle was the grip of an oversize wide-toothed comb. She'd sit at her desk with her book unopened, and when the teacher asked her to turn to page thirty-six, she'd mutter she wasn't opening nothing to no damn page thirty-six or two hundred neither.

"Did you say something, Debra?"

"No, ma'am," she'd answer, followed by a closemouthed, almost inaudible, "Hell, yeah, I said something. Take your ugly head outcha ass and maybe you can hear it."

"I'm sorry, but is there a problem?"

"No." Then, "Yeah, bitch, *you* my problem."

Delicia, by contrast, was timid and sweet, with short Afroed hair and a soft, almost childlike voice. I thought that because she was shy she'd be a good student, but those two things didn't always go together. She was polite, certainly, and seemed to try as hard as she could. It just wasn't good enough for the north side. The two of us were in the same English class, and though I told myself that we were friends, her reticence made it hard to hold any kind of real conversation. Like all the new kids, she used the word "stay" in place of "live," as in "I stay on South Saunders Street," or "I stay in Chavis Heights." Delicia stayed with her aunt, which she pronounced to rhyme with "taunt."

That was all I knew about her personal life. Everything else was my own invention. I decided for a start that she was virtuous and eager to change, that our association was, in some substantial way, improving her. It's not how a person would think of an actual friend, much less a potential girlfriend. This was the status I upgraded her to a few weeks into the school year. At fourteen, I figured it was about time I took the plunge. Everyone kept asking if I was going steady, or at least everyone creepy kept asking, particularly the men from the Greek Orthodox church, who'd refer even to newborn babies as "lady-killers" and wonder how many hearts they had broken. Like it wasn't enough to be dating at the age of three weeks, you also had to be two-timing someone.

To the other boys in my Sunday school class, it was "Who's the lucky lady?" To me it was just "Find anyone yet?" And though at that age I never could have admitted it, I was as physically attracted to Delicia as I'd have been to any female. Her body was no less appealing to me than that of our head cheerleader, so why *not* have the two-hundred-fifty-pound girlfriend from the wrong side of town?

The idea coincided with my Greek grandmother's moving from our house into a new senior citizens' apartment complex called Capital Towers. She was cruelly out of place there, the only resident who wasn't born in the United States and who didn't try, in that resolutely American way, to be gay and youthful. Where Yiayiá was from, old age was not something to be disguised or outrun. Rather, you embraced it, and gratefully, for decrepitude, in Greece, was not without its benefits. There, you lived in a compound with your extended family, and everyone younger than you became your pawn. In America, being old got you nothing but a spare bedroom that was painted purple and had bumper stickers on the door. Then one day your daughter-in-law decides she's had enough, and out you go, not just to an apartment but to *a studio* apartment, which basically means a bedroom with a kitchen in it.

Capital Towers was trying to get an activities program going. A social was to be held on a Sunday afternoon in early October, and that, I decided, was just the place to take Delicia on our first date.

"You've got to be kidding me," my mother said.

"No," I told her. "I think it would be interesting for her to meet Yiayiá."

"*Interesting?*" My mother allowed her tone of voice to do the heavy lifting, as unless you were making a documentary about gloom, there was nothing interesting about my grandmother. Or at least not to us at the time. If I could go back to 1972, and if I were able to understand Greek, she might have told me all sorts of fascinating things: what it was like to endure a loveless arranged marriage, to be traded away by your family and forced to sail to another country. From Ellis Island, she went to Cortland, New York, a little town in the western part of the state. There, she and her pitiless husband opened a newsstand not much larger than their cash box. What was it like to forfeit your youth? To be illiterate in two languages? To lose every tooth in your head by the age of forty? All I really knew was that Yiayiá loved us. Not in a *specific* way—she could no sooner name our good qualities than the cat could— yet still we could feel it. I'd occasionally allow her to stroke my hand. All us kids would from time to time, and all of us thought of it as work. Oh, how exhausting it was to let someone adore you.

My Yiayiá was exactly the sort of friend I'd have liked as an adult, someone with an endless supply of hard-luck stories and no desire to ever write a book. At the time, though, she was just an obligation. If I had to go to the social, I figured I might as well get something out of it—hence bringing Delicia. All we'd have to do was walk in holding hands, and the old people would freak out, no one more so than my grandmother. "Who the blackie?" she'd likely ask, for that was the word she continued to use, no matter how often we shouted "Negro" at her.

"I'm not having any part of it," my mother said.

"So you won't even give us a ride?"

When she told me no, I accused her of being prejudiced. "You just don't want your son dating a girl who's not white."

She said she didn't care who I dated but that I was not going to bring this Delicia person to Capital Towers.

"Fine, then, I'll bring her to church."

"You're not bringing her there either," my mother told me. "It's not fair to *her*."

"You object to anyone who's not like you!" I yelled. "You're just afraid your grandchildren will be half black."

How I'd jumped from dragging some poor girl to a senior citizens' apartment complex to dating her and then to fathering her children is beyond me now, but my mother, who by then had three teenagers and three more coming right behind them, took it in stride.

"That's right," she said. "I want you to marry someone exactly like me, with a big beige purse and lots of veins in her legs. In fact, why don't I just divorce your father so the two of us can run off together?"

"You're disgusting," I told her. "I'll *never* marry you. *Never!*" I left the room in a great, dramatic huff, thinking, *Did I just refuse to marry my mother?*

and then, secretly, *I'm free!* The part of my plan that made old people uncomfortable, that exposed them for the bigots they were—and on a Sunday!—still appealed to me. But the mechanics of it would have been a pain. Buses wouldn't be running, so someone would have to drive to the south side, pick up Delicia, and then come back across town. After I'd finished shocking everyone, I'd have to somehow get her home. I didn't imagine her aunt had a car. My mother wasn't going to drive us, so that just left my dad, who would certainly be watching football and wouldn't leave his spot in front of the TV even if my date was white and offered to chip in for the gas. Surely something could be arranged, but it seemed easier to take the out that had just been handed to me and to say that our date was forbidden.

Love seemed all the sweeter when it was misunderstood, condemned by the outside world. The thing about Delicia was that we barely knew each other. Her interest in me was pure conjecture, based not on anything she'd said or done but on my cruel assumption that no one else would be interested in her. Our most intimate conversation took place when I unbuttoned my shirt one afternoon and showed her what I was hiding beneath it: a T-shirt that pictured a male goose mounted, midair, on a female, his tongue drooping from his bill in an expression of satisfied exhaustion. "See"—and I pointed to the words written across my chest—"it says 'Fly United.'"

Delicia blinked.

"That's an airline," I told her.

"You crazy," she said.

"Yes, well, that's me!"

On the Monday after the social, I broke it to Delicia that I'd wanted to take her somewhere special but that my parents hadn't allowed it. "I hate them," I told her. "They're so prejudiced you wouldn't believe it."

I don't know what response I expected, but a show of disappointment would have been a good start. If this relationship was going to take off, we needed a common cause, but that, it seemed, was not going to happen. All she said was "That's okay."

"Well, no, actually, it's not okay," I told her. "Actually it stinks." I laid my hand over hers on the desktop and then looked down at it, thinking what a great poster this would make. "Togetherness," it might read. I'd expected electricity to pass mutually between us, but all I really felt was self-conscious, and disappointed that more people weren't looking on.

As for Delicia, what goes through a person's mind the first time they're patronized? Was she embarrassed? Enraged? Or perhaps this wasn't her first time. Maybe it happened so often she'd simply resigned herself to it.

It's a start, I thought as I lifted my hand off hers and turned around in my seat. I figured we had our entire lives ahead of us, but by Thanksgiving I'd been accepted into a crowd of midlevel outcasts and had pretty much forgotten about her. We still said hello to each other, but we never ate lunch together or talked on the phone or did any of the things that real friends did. I don't recall seeing her in the later grades and am not sure if she attended my high school or if she stayed on her side of town and went to Enloe. It must have been a good seven years before I saw her again. I had dropped out of my second college and was working as a furniture refinisher not far from downtown Raleigh. There was a dime store I'd pass on my bike ride home each day, and I looked up one afternoon to see Delicia walking out the front door. She had a name tag on and a smock, and when I stopped to say hello she seemed to genuinely remember me.

"So, are you the manager of this place?" I asked.

And she said, "You crazy."

I'd like to think that Delicia managing a dime store was not on the same level as a T-shirt reading "Fly United," so her response saddened me. My invented version of her was pragmatic and responsible, but all I really knew was that she was nice and shy, and apparently still poor. By this time we were in our twenties, and I understood that friendship could not be manufactured. You didn't look through your address book thinking, *Where are the Koreans?* or *I need to meet more paralyzed people.* Not that it's outlandish to have such friends, but they have to be made organically.

The people I hung out with in my early twenties were middle-class and, at least to our minds, artistic. We'd all turned our backs on privilege, but comfortably, the way you can when you still have access to it. No one wanted to call home asking for money, but we all knew that in a pinch our parents would come through for us. It was this, more than race, that set me apart from Delicia, for how could someone on the bottom rung of the ladder not be outraged by the unfairness of it all?

Passing the dime store on subsequent afternoons, I'd think of my family's former maid, Lena, who started working for us when my brother was born and stayed until my grandmother moved out. She and my mom spent a lot of time talking, and though my mother, like all the mothers on our street, thought of her housekeeper as a friend, I knew that what she really meant was "a person I pay and am on good terms with." For how many mothers hung out with *other* people's maids? What would the O'Connors have thought if my mom showed up at their door with a canteen around her neck? "Is Marthandra off work yet? I thought the two of us might try camping this weekend."

Maybe in a tent, away from the cars and color TVs and air-conditioning, a friendship could have taken root. As it was, there was just too much in-equality to overcome. If you want a friend whose life is the economic opposite of your own, it seems your best bet is to find a pen pal, the type you normally get in grade school. This is someone who writes from afar to tell you that his dromedary escaped. You respond that your bike has a flat tire, and he answers that in his country August is a time for feasting. It's all done through the mail, so he never sees your new suburban house, and you never see the hubcap his family uses to boil water in. Plus, you're a kid, so your first thought isn't *Yuck, a dromedary,* but

Wow, a dromedary! Or a raccoon, or a mongoose, or a honey badger.

As weeks passed and the cell phone salesman didn't call back, I started worrying that he'd lost his job. Maybe, though, that's just me being a cultural elitist, assuming that his life must go from bad to worse. Isn't it just as likely that he got promoted or, better still, that he left the call center for greener pastures? *That's it,* I tell myself. *Once he settles into the new job and moves into that house he's been eyeing, after his maid has left for the day and he's figured out which remote works the television and which one is for the DVD player, he's going to need someone to relate to. Then he'll dig up my number, reach for his cell phone, and, by God, call me.*

Loggerheads

The thing about Hawaii, at least the part that is geared toward tourists, is that it's exactly what it promises to be. Step off the plane, and someone places a lei around your neck, as if it were something you had earned—an Olympic medal for sitting on your ass. Raise a hand above your shoulder and, no matter where you are, a drink will appear: something served in a hollowed-out pineapple, or perhaps in a coconut that's been sawed in half. *Just like in the time before glasses!* you think.

Volcanic craters, waterfalls, and those immaculate beaches—shocking things when you're coming from Europe. At the spot Hugh and I go to in Normandy you'll find, in place of sand, speckled stones the size of potatoes. The water runs from glacial to heart attack and is tinted the color of iced tea. Then there's all the stuff floating in it: not man-made garbage but sea garbage—scum and bits of plant life, all of it murky and rotten-smelling.

The beaches in Hawaii look as if they've been

bleached; that's how white the sand is. The water is warm—even in winter—and so clear you can see not just your toes but the corns cleaving, barnacle-like, to the sides of them. On Maui, one November, Hugh and I went swimming, and turned to find a gigantic sea turtle coming up between us. As gentle as a cow, she was, and with a cow's dopey, almost lovesick expression on her face. That, to me, was worth the entire trip, worth my entire life, practically. For to witness majesty, to find yourself literally touched by it—isn't that what we've all been waiting for?

I had a similar experience a few years later, and again with Hugh. We were in Japan, walking through a national forest in a snowstorm, when a monkey the height of a bar stool brushed against us. His fur was a dull silver, the color of dishwater, but he had this beet-red face, set in a serious, almost solemn expression. We saw it full-on when he turned to briefly look at us. Then he shrugged and ambled off over a footbridge.

"Jesus Christ!" I said. Because it was all too much: the forest, the snowstorm, and now this. Monkeys are an attraction in that part of the country. We expected to see them at some point, but I thought they'd be fenced in. As with the sea turtle, part of the thrill was the feeling of being accepted, which is to say, not feared. It allowed you to think that you and this creature had a special relationship, a juvenile thought but one that brings with it a definite comfort. *Well, monkeys like me,* I'd find myself thinking during the next few months, whenever I felt lonely or unappreciated. Just as, in the months following our trip to Hawaii, I thought of the sea turtle. With her, though, my feelings were a bit more complicated, and instead of believing that we had bonded, I'd wonder that she could ever have forgiven me.

The thing between me and sea turtles started in the late '60s, and involved my best friend from grade school, a boy I'll call Shaun, who lived down the street from me in Raleigh. What brought us together was a love of nature, or, more specifically, of catching things and unintentionally killing them. We started when I was in the fourth grade, which would have made me ten, I guess. It's different for everyone, but at that age, though I couldn't have said that I was gay, I knew that I was not like the other boys in my class or my Scout troop. While they welcomed male company, I shrank from it, dreaded it, feeling like someone forever trying to pass, someone who would eventually be found out, and expelled from polite society. *Is this how a normal boy would swing his arms?* I'd ask myself, standing before the full-length mirror in my parents' bedroom. *Is this how he'd laugh? Is this what he would find funny?* It was like doing an English accent. The more concentrated the attempt, the more self-conscious and unconvincing I became.

    With Shaun, though, I could almost be myself. This didn't mean that we were alike, only that he wasn't paying that much attention. Childhood, for him, seemed something to be endured, passed through like a tiresome stretch of road. Ahead of this was the good stuff, and looking at him from time to time, at the way he had of staring off, of boring a hole into the horizon, you got the sense that he could not only imagine it but actually see it: this great grown-up life, waiting on the other side of sixteen.

Apart from an interest in wildlife, the two of us shared an identity as transplants. My family was from the North, and the Taylors were from the Midwest. Shaun's father, Hank, was a psychiatrist and sometimes gave his boys and me tests, the type for which there were, he assured us, "no right answers." He and his wife were younger than my parents, and they seemed it, not just in their dress but in their eclectic tastes—records by Donovan and Moby Grape shelved among the Schubert. Their house had real hardcover books in it, and you often saw them lying open on the sofa, the words still warm from being read.

In a neighborhood of stay-at-home moms, Shaun's mother worked. A public-health nurse, she was the one you went to if you woke up with yellow eyes or jammed a piece of caramel corn too far into your ear. "Oh, you're fine," Jean would say, for that was what she wanted us to call her, not Mrs. Taylor. With her high cheekbones and ever so slightly turned-down mouth, she brought to mind a young Katharine Hepburn. Other mothers might be pretty, might, in their twenties or early thirties, *pause* at beauty, but Jean was clearly parked there for a lifetime. You'd see her in her flower bed, gardening gloves hanging from the waistband of her slacks like someone clawing to get out, and you just had to wish she was your mom instead.

The Taylor children had inherited their mother's good looks, especially Shaun. Even as a kid he seemed at home in his skin—never cute, just handsome, blond hair like a curtain drawn over half his face. The eye that looked out the uncurtained side was cornflower blue, and excelled at spotting wounded or vulnerable animals. While the other boys in our neighborhood played touch football in the street, Shaun and I searched the woods behind our houses. I drew the line at snakes, but anything else was brought home and imprisoned in our ten-gallon aquariums. Lizards, toads, baby birds: they all got the same diet—raw hamburger meat—and, with few exceptions, they all died within a week or two.

"Menu-wise, it might not hurt you to branch out a little," my mother once said, in reference to my captive luna moth. It was the size of a paperback novel, a beautiful mint green, but not much interested in ground chuck. "Maybe you could feed it some, I don't know, flowers or something."

Like she knew.

The best-caught creature belonged to Shaun's younger brother, Chris, who'd found an injured flying squirrel and kept him, uncaged, in his bedroom. The thing was no bigger than an ordinary hamster, and when he glided from the top bunk to the dresser, his body flattened out, making him look like an empty hand puppet. The only problem was the squirrel's disposition, his one-track mind. You wanted him to cuddle or ride sentry on your shoulder, but he refused to relax. *I've got to get out of here,* you could sense him thinking, as he clawed, desperate and wild-eyed, at the windowpane, or tried to squeeze himself underneath the door. He made it out eventually, and though we all hoped he'd return for meals, become a kind of part-time pet, he never did.

Not long after the squirrel broke free, Jean took her boys and me for a weekend on the North Carolina coast. It was mid-October, the start of the sixth grade, and the water was too chilly to swim in. On the Sunday we were to head back home, Shaun and I got up at dawn and took a walk with our nets. We were hunting for ghost crabs, when in the distance we made out these creatures moving blockily, like windup toys on an unsteady surface. On closer inspection we saw that they were baby sea turtles, dozens of them, digging out from under the sand and stumbling toward the ocean.

An adult might have carried them into the surf, or held at bay the predatory gulls, but we were twelve, so while I scooped the baby turtles into a pile, Shaun ran back and got the trash cans from our hotel room. We might have walked off with the whole lot, but they seemed pretty miserable, jumbled atop one another. Thus, in the end, we took just ten, which meant five apiece.

The great thing about the sea turtles, as opposed to, say, flying squirrels, was that they would grow exponentially—meaning, what, fifty, a hundred

times their original size? When we got them, each
called to mind a plastic coin purse, the oval sort
handed out by banks and car dealerships. Then there
were the flippers and, of course, the heads, which
were bald and beaky, like a newly hatched bird's.
Since the death of a traumatized mole pried from the
mouth of our cat, Samantha, my aquarium had sat
empty and was therefore ready for some new tenants.
I filled it with a jug of ocean water I'd brought from
the beach, then threw in a conch shell and a couple
of sand dollars to make it more homey. The turtles
swam the short distance from one end of the tank to
the other, and then they batted at the glass with their
flippers, unable to understand that this was it—the
end of the road. What they needed, it seemed, was
something to eat.

"Mom, do we have any raw hamburger?"

Looking back, you'd think that someone would
have said something—sea turtles, for God's sake!—
but maybe they weren't endangered yet. Animal cru-
elty hadn't been invented either. The thought that
a non–human being had *physical* feelings, let alone
the wherewithal to lose hope, was outlandish and
alien, like thinking that paper had relatives. Then
too, when it comes to eliciting empathy, it's the back
of the line for reptiles and amphibians, creatures
with, face it, not much in the way of a personality.
Even giving them names didn't help, as playing with
Shelly was no different from playing with Pokyhon-
tus; "playing," in this case, amounting to placing
them on my desk and watching them toddle over the
edge.

It was good to know that in the house down the street Shaun's turtles weren't faring much better. The hamburger meat we'd put in our aquariums went uneaten, and within a short time it spoiled and started stinking up our rooms. I emptied my tank, and in the absence of more seawater, I made my own with plain old tap water and salt.

"I'm not sure that that's going to work," my mother said. She was standing in my doorway with a cigarette in one hand and an ashtray in the other. Recent experiments with a home-frosting kit had dried out and broken her already brittle hair. What was left she'd covered with a scarf, a turquoise one, that looked great when she had a tan but not so great when she didn't. "Doesn't ocean water have nutrients in it or something?"

"I dunno."

She looked at the turtles unhappily dragging themselves across my bedspread. "Well, if you want to find out, I'm taking Lisa to the library this Saturday."

I'd hoped to spend my weekend outside, but then it rained and my father hogged the TV for one of his football games. It was either go to the library or stay home and die of boredom, so I got into the car, groaning at the unfairness of it all. My mother dropped my sister and me downtown, and then she went to do some shopping, promising to return in a few hours.

It wasn't much to look at, our public library. I'd later learn that it used to be a department store, which made sense: the floor-to-ceiling windows were right for mannequins, and you could easily imagine dress shirts where the encyclopedias were, wigs in place of the magazines. I remember that in the basement there were two restrooms, one marked "Men" and the other marked "Gentlemen." Inside each was a toilet, a sink, and a paper towel dispenser, meaning that whichever you chose you got pretty much the same treatment. Thus it came down to how you saw yourself: as regular or fancy. On the day I went to research turtles, I saw myself as fancy, so I opened the door marked "Gentlemen." What happened next happened very quickly: Two men, both of them black, turned their heads in my direction. One was standing with his pants and underwear pulled down past his knees, and as he bent to yank them up, the other man, who'd been kneeling before him and who also had his pants lowered, covered his face with his hand and let out a little cry.

"Oh," I told them, "I'm sorry."

I backed, shaken, out of the room, and just as the door had closed behind me, it swung open again. Then the pair spilled out, that flying-squirrel look in their eyes. The stairs were at the end of a short hall, and they took them two at a time, the slower man turning his head, just briefly, and looking at me as if I held a gun. When I saw that he was afraid of me, I felt powerful. Then I wondered how I might use that power.

My first instinct was to tell on them—not because I wanted the two punished but because I would have liked the attention. "Are you all right?" the librarian would have asked. "And these were Negroes, you say? Quick, somebody, get this young man a glass of water or, better yet, a Coke. Would you like a Coke while we wait for the police?"

And in my feeblest voice I would have said, "Yes."

Then again, it could so easily backfire. The men were doing something indecent, and recognizing it as such meant that I had an eye for it. That I too was suspect. And wasn't I?

In the end I told no one. Not even Lisa.

"So did you find out what kind of turtles they are?" my mother asked as we climbed back into the car.

"Sea turtles," I told her.

"Well, we *know* that."

"No, I mean, that's what they're called, 'sea turtles.'"

"And what do they eat?"

I looked out the rain-streaked window. "Hamburger."

My mother sighed. "Have it your way."

It took a few weeks for my first turtle to die. The water in the tank had again grown murky with spoiled, uneaten beef, but there was something else as well, something I couldn't begin to identify. The smell that developed in the days after Halloween, this deep, swampy funk, was enough to make your throat close up. It was as if the turtles' very souls were rotting, yet still they gathered in the corner of their tank, determined to find the sea. At night I would hear their flippers against the glass, and think about the

Negroes in the Gentlemen's room, wondering what would become of them—what, by extension, would become of me? Would I too have to live on the run? Afraid of even a twelve-year-old?

One Friday in early November my father paid a rare visit to my room. In his hand was a glass of gin, his standard after-work cocktail, mixed with a little water and garnished with a lemon peel. I liked the drink's medicinal smell, but today it was overpowered by the aquarium. He regarded it briefly and, wincing at the stench, removed two tickets from his jacket pocket. "They're for a game," he told me.

"A game?"

"Football," he said. "I thought we could go tomorrow afternoon."

"But tomorrow I have to write a report."

"Write it on Sunday."

I'd never expressed any interest in football. Never played it with the kids on the street, never watched it on TV, never touched the helmet I'd received the previous Christmas. "Why not take Lisa?" I asked.

"Because you're my son, that's why."

I looked at the holocaust taking place in my aquarium. "Do I have to?"

If I were to go to a game today, I'd certainly find something to enjoy: the food, the noise, the fans marked up with paint. It would be an experience. At the time, though, it threw me into a panic. *Which team am I supposed to care about?* I asked myself as we settled into our seats. *How should I react if somebody scores a point?* The thing about sports, at least for guys, is that nobody ever defines the rules, not even in gym class. Asking what a penalty means is like asking who Jesus was. It's one of those things you're just supposed to know, and if you don't, there's something seriously wrong with you.

Two of the popular boys from my school were standing against a railing a few rows ahead of us, and when I stupidly pointed them out to my father, he told me to go say hello.

How to explain that looking at them, even from this distance, was pushing it. Addressing them, it followed, was completely out of the question. People had their places, and to not understand that, to act in violation of it, demoted you from a nature nut to something even lower, a complete untouchable, basically. "That's all right," I said. "They don't really know who I am."

"Aw, baloney. Go over and talk to them."

"No, really."

"Do you want me to drag you over there?"

As I dug in, I thought of the turtles. All they'd ever wanted was to live in the ocean—that was it, their entire wish list, and instead I'd decided they'd be better off in my bedroom. Just as my dad had decided that I'd be better off at the football game. If I could have returned them to the beach, I would have, though I knew it was already too late. In another few days they would start going blind. Then their shells would soften, and they'd just sort of melt away, like soap.

"Are you going over there or aren't you?" my dad said.

*   *   *

When the last turtle died and was pitched into the woods behind my house, Shaun and I took up bowling, the only sport I was ever half decent at. The Western Lanes was a good distance away, and when our parents wouldn't drive us, we rode our bikes, me with a transistor radio attached by rubber bands to my handlebars. We were just thinking of buying our own bowling shoes when Shaun's mother and father separated. Hank took an apartment in one of the new complexes, and a few months later, not yet forty years old, he died.

"Died of what?" I asked.

"His heart stopped beating" was the answer Shaun gave me.

"Well, sure," I said, "but doesn't *every* dead person's heart stop beating? There must have been something else going on."

"His heart stopped beating."

Following the funeral there was a reception at the Taylors' house. Shaun and I spent most of it on the deck off his living room, him firing his BB gun into the woods with that telescopic look in his eye. After informing me that his father's heart had stopped beating, he never said another word about him. I never saw Shaun cry, or buckle at the knees, or do any of the things that I would have done. Dramawise it was the chance of a lifetime, but he wasn't having any of it. From the living room, I could hear my father talking to Jean. "What with Hank gone, the boys are going to need a positive male influence in their lives," he said. "That being the case, I'll be happy to, well, happy to—"

"Ignore them," my mother cut in. "Just like he does with his own damn kids."

And Jean laughed. "Oh, Sharon."

Eighteen years passed before I learned what had really happened to Shaun's father. By then I was living in Chicago. My parents were still in Raleigh, and several times a week I'd talk to my mother on the phone. I don't remember how the subject came up, but after she told me I was stunned.

"Did Shaun know?" I asked.

"I'm sure he did," my mother said, and although I hadn't seen or spoken to him since high school, I couldn't help but feel a little betrayed. If you can't tell your best friend that your dad essentially drank himself to death, who *can* you tell? It's a lot to hold in at that age, but then I guess we all had our secrets.

It was after talking to my mom on the phone that I finally went to the library and looked up those turtles: "loggerheads" is what they were called. When mature, they can measure three and a half feet long. A female might reach four hundred pounds, and, of all the eggs she lays in a lifetime, only one in a thousand will make it to adulthood. Pretty slim odds when, by "making it," you mean simply surviving.

Before the reception ended that day, Shaun handed his BB gun to me. My father was watching from the living room window and interceded just as I raised it to my shoulder.

"Oh no, you don't. You're going to put somebody's eye out."

"Somebody like a bird?" I said. "We're firing into the woods, not into the house."

"I don't give a damn where you're aiming."

I handed the rifle back to Shaun, and as he brushed the hair from his eyes and peered down the scope, I tried to see what I imagined he did: a life on the other side of this, something better, perhaps even majestic, waiting for us to grow into it.

If I Ruled the World

If I ruled the world, the first thing I'd do is concede all power to the *real* King, who, in case you don't happen to know, is named Jesus Christ. A lot of people have managed to forget this lately, so the second thing I'd do is remind them of it. Not only would I bring back mandatory prayer in school, but I'd also institute it at work. Then in skating rinks and airports. Wherever people live or do business, they shall know His name. Christ's picture will go on all our money, and if you had your checks specially printed with sailboats or shamrocks on them, too bad for you because from here on out, the only images allowed will be of Him, or maybe of me reminding you of how important He is.

T-shirts with crosses and apostles on them will be allowed, but none of this nonsense you see nowadays, this one my neighbor has, for example. "Certified Sex Instructor," it says. He claims he only wears it while mowing the lawn, but in the summer that's once a week, which in my book is once a week too often. I mean, please, he's seventy-two!

Jesus and I are going to take that T-shirt, and all the ones like it, and use them as rags for washing people's mouths out. I normally don't believe in rough stuff, but what about those who simply refuse to learn? "Look," I'll say to Jesus, "enough is enough. I suggest we nail some boards together and have ourselves an old-fashioned crucifixion." It's bound to stir up a few bad memories, but having been gone for all that time, He probably won't know how bad things have gotten. "Just turn on the radio," I'll tell Him. "It's the thing next to my ferret cage with all the knobs on it."

Jesus will tune in to our local so-called music station, and within two minutes He'll know what I'm talking about—music so rude it'll make His ears blister. And the TV! I turned mine on the other morning and came upon a man who used to be a woman. Had a little mustache, a potbelly and everything. Changed her name from Mary Louise to Vince and sat back with a satisfied smile on her face, figuring she'd licked the system. And maybe she did last year when they did the operation, but Jesus is the system now, and we'll just have to hear what He has to say about it.

The creature on TV—I can't say male or female without bringing on a stomachache—said that when it was a woman it was attracted to men and that it still is. This means that now, on top of everything else, it's a homosexual. As if we didn't have enough already, some doctor had to go and *make* one!

Well, to hell with him—quite literally—and to hell with all the other gays too. And the abortionists, and the people who have had abortions, even if they were raped or the baby had three heads and delivering it was going to tear the mother to pieces. "That was YOUR baby," I'm going to say to Jesus. "Now, are you going to just sit there and watch it get thrown onto some trash heap?"

And Jesus will say, "No, Cassie Hasselback, I am not!"

He and I are going to work really well together. "What's next on the agenda?" He'll ask, and I'll point Him to the Muslims and vegans who believe their God is the real one. The same goes for the Buddhists and whoever it is that thinks cows and monkeys have special powers. Then we'll move on to the comedians, with their "F this" and "GD that." I'll crucify the Democrats, the Communists, and a good 97 percent of the college students. Don't laugh, Tim Cobblestone, because you're next! Think you can let your cat foul my flower beds and get away with it? Well, think again! And Curtis Devlin, who turned down my application for a home-improvement loan; and Carlotta Buffington, who only got her job because she's paralyzed on one side; and even my grandson Kenyan Bullock. He just turned five, but no matter what Trisha says, this is not a phase—the child is evil, and it's best to stop him now before any real damage is done. And all the other evil people and whores and liars who want to take away our freedom or raise my taxes, they shall know our fury, Jesus's and mine, and burn forever.

Easy, Tiger

On a recent flight from Tokyo to Beijing, at around the time that my lunch tray was taken away, I remembered that I needed to learn Mandarin. "Goddamnit," I whispered. "I knew I forgot something."

Normally, when landing in a foreign country, I'm prepared to say, at the very least, "Hello," and "I'm sorry." This trip, though, was a two-parter, and I'd used my month of prep time to bone up on my Japanese. For this, I returned to the Pimsleur audio program I'd relied on for my previous two visits. I'd used its Italian version as well and had noted that they followed the same basic pattern. In the first thirty-minute lesson, a man approaches a strange woman, asking, in Italian or Japanese or whichever language you've signed up for, if she understands English. The two jabber away for twenty seconds or so, and then an American instructor chimes in and breaks it all down. "Say, 'Excuse me,'" he tells you. "Ask, 'Are you an American?'" The conversations grow more complicated as you progress, and the phrases are regularly repeated so that you don't forget them.

Not all the sentences I've learned with Pimsleur are suited to my way of life. I don't drive, for example, so "Which is the road to go to Yokohama?" never did me any good. The same is true of "As for gas, is it expensive?" though I have got some mileage out of "Fill her up, please," which I use in restaurants when getting a second cup of tea.

Thanks to Japanese I and II, I'm able to buy train tickets, count to nine hundred and ninety-nine thousand, and say, whenever someone is giving me change, "Now you are giving me change." I can manage in a restaurant, take a cab, and even make small talk with the driver. "Do you have children?" I ask. "Will you take a vacation this year?" "Where to?" When he turns it around, as Japanese cabdrivers are inclined to do, I tell him that I have three children, a big boy and two little girls. If Pimsleur included "I am a middle-aged homosexual and thus make do with a niece I never see and a very small godson," I'd say that. In the meantime, I work with what I have.

Pimsleur's a big help when it comes to pronunciation. The actors are native speakers, and they don't slow down for your benefit. The drawbacks are that they never explain anything or teach you to think for yourself. Instead of being provided with building blocks that would allow you to construct a sentence of your own, you're left with using the hundreds or thousands of sentences that you have memorized. That means waiting for a particular situation to arise in order to comment on it; either that, or becoming one of those weird non-sequitur people, the kind who, when asked a question about paint color, answer, "There is a bank in front of the train station," or, "Mrs. Yamada Ito has been playing tennis for fifteen years."

I hadn't downloaded a Pimsleur program for China, so on the flight to Beijing I turned to my Lonely Planet phrase book, knowing it was hopeless. Mandarin is closer to singing than it is to talking, and even though the words were written phonetically, I couldn't begin to get the hang of them. The book was slim and palm-size, divided into short chapters: "Banking," "Shopping," "Border Crossing." The one titled "Romance" included the following: "Would you like a drink?" "You're a fantastic dancer." "You look like some cousin of mine." The latter would work only if you were Asian, but even then it's a little creepy, the implication being "the cousin I have always wanted to undress and ejaculate on."

In the subchapter "Getting Closer," one learns to say, "I like you very much." "You're great." "Do you want a massage?" On the following page, things heat up. "I want you." "I want to make love to you." "How about going to bed?" And, a line that might have been written especially for me, "Don't worry, I'll do it myself."

Oddly, the writers haven't included "Leave the light on," a must if you want to actually *say* any of these things. One pictures the vacationer naked on a bed and squinting into his or her little book to moan,

"Oh yeah!" "Easy, tiger," "Faster," "Harder," "Slower," "Softer." "That was...amazing/weird/wild." "Can I stay over?"

In the following subchapter, it all falls apart: "Are you seeing someone else?" "He/she is just a friend." "You're just using me for sex." "I don't think it's working out." And, finally, "I never want to see you again."

Hugh and I returned from China, and a few days later I started preparing for a trip to Germany. The first time I went, in 1999, I couldn't bring myself to say so much as *"Guten Morgen."* The sounds felt false coming out of my mouth, so instead I spent my time speaking English apologetically. Not that the apologies were needed. In Paris, yes, but in Berlin people's attitude is "Thank you for allowing me to practice my perfect English." And I do mean perfect. "Are you from Minnesota?" I kept asking.

In the beginning, I was put off by the harshness of German. Someone would order a piece of cake, and it sounded as if it were an actual order, like, "Cut the cake and lie facedown in that ditch between the cobbler and the little girl." I'm guessing this comes from having watched too many Second World War movies. Then I remembered the umpteen Fassbinder films I sat through in the '80s, and German began to sound conflicted instead of heartless. I went back twice in 2000, and over time the language grew on me. It's like English, but sideways.

I've made at least ten separate trips by now and

have gone from one end of the country to the other. People taught me all sorts of words, but the only ones that stuck were *"Kaiserschnitt,"* which means "cesarean section," and *"Lebensabschnittspartner."* This doesn't translate to "lover" or "life partner" but, rather, to "the person I am with today," the implication being that things change, and you are keeping yourself open.

For this latest trip, I wanted to do better, so I downloaded all thirty lessons of Pimsleur German I, which again start off with "Excuse me, do you understand English?" As with the Japanese and the Italian versions, the program taught me to count and to tell time. Again I learned "The girl is already big" and "How are you?" (*"Wie geht es Ihnen?"*)

In Japanese and Italian, the response to the final question is "I'm fine, and you?" In German it's answered with a sigh and a slight pause, followed by "Not so good."

I mentioned this to my German friend Tilo, who said that of course that was the response. "We can't get it through our heads that people are asking only to be polite," he said.

In Japanese I, lesson 17, the actress who plays the wife says, *"Kaimono ga shitai n desu ga!"* ("I want to go shopping, but there's a problem and you need to guess what it is.") The exercise is about numbers, so the husband asks how much money she has. She gives him a figure, and he offers to increase it incrementally.

Similarly, in the German version, the wife announces that she wants to buy something: *"Ich möchte noch etwas kaufen.*" Her husband asks how much money she has, and after she answers, he responds coldly, "I'm not giving you any more. You have enough."

There's no discord in Pimsleur's Japan, but its Germany is a moody and often savage place. In one of the exercises, you're encouraged to argue with a bellhop who tries to cheat you out of your change and who ends up sneering, "You don't understand German."

"Oh, but I do," you learn to say. "I *do* understand German."

It's a program full of odd sentence combinations. "We don't live here. We want mineral water" implies that if the couple *did* live in this particular town they'd be getting drunk like everyone else. Another standout is *"Der Wein ist zu teuer und Sie sprechen zu schnell."* ("The wine is too expensive and you talk too fast.") The response to this would be "Anything else, Herr Asshole?" But of course they don't teach you that.

On our last trip to Tokyo, Hugh and I rented an apartment in a nondescript neighborhood a few subway stops from Shinjuku Station. A representative from the real estate agency met us at the front door, and when I spoke to him in Japanese, he told me I needed to buy myself some manga. "Read those and you'll learn how people actually talk," he said. "You, you're a little too polite."

I know what he was getting at, but I really don't

see this as much of a problem, especially if you're a foreigner and any perceived rudeness can turn someone not just against you but against your entire country. Here Pimsleur has it all over the phrase books of my youth, where the Ugly American was still alive and kicking people. "I didn't order this!" he raged in Greek and Spanish. "Think you can cheat me, do you?" "Go away or I'll call the police."

Now for the traveling American there's less of a need for phrase books. Not only do we expect everyone to speak our language; we expect everyone to be fluent. I rarely hear an American vacationer say to a waiter or shopkeeper in Europe, "Your English is so good." Rather, we act as if it were part of his job, like carrying a tray or making change. In this respect, the phrase books and audio programs are an almost charming throwback, a suggestion that *the traveler* put himself out there, that *he* open himself to criticism and not the person who's just trying to scrape by selling meatballs in Bumfucchio, Italy.

One of the things I like about Tokyo is the constant reinforcement one gets for trying. "You are very skilled at Japanese," everyone keeps telling me. I know people are just being polite, but it spurs me on, just as I hoped to be spurred on in Germany. To this end, I've added a second audio program, one by a man named Michel Thomas, who works with a couple of students, a male and a female. At the start, he explains that German and English are closely related and thus have a lot in common. In one language, the verb is "to come," and in the other it's *"kommen."* English "to give" is German *"geben."*

Boston's "That is good" is Berlin's *"Das ist gut."*
It's an excellent way to start and leaves the listener
thinking, *Hey, Ich kann do dis.*

Unlike the nameless instructor in Pimsleur, Herr
Thomas explains things—the fact, for example, that
if there are two verbs in a German sentence, one of
them comes at the end. He doesn't give you phrases
to memorize. In fact, he actively discourages study.
"How would you say, 'Give it to me?'" he asks the
female student. She and I correctly answer, and then
he turns to the male. "Now try 'I would like for you
to give it to me.'"

Ten minutes later, we've graduated to "I can't give
it to you today, because I cannot find it." To people
who speak nothing but English, this might seem easy
enough, but anyone else will appreciate how difficult it is: negatives, multiple uses of "it," and the hell
that breaks loose following the German "because."
The thrill is that you're actually figuring it out on
your own. You're engaging with another language,
not just parroting it.

Walking through the grocery store with Pimsleur
und Thomas on my iPod, I picture myself pulling up
to my Munich hotel with my friend Ulrike, who's
only ever known me to say "cesarean section" and
"the person I am with until someone better comes
along."

"Bleiben wir hier heute Abend?" I plan to say.
"Wieviele Nächte? Zwei? Das ist teuer, nicht wahr?"

She's a wonderful woman, Ulrike, and if that's all

I get out of this—seeing the shock register on her face as I natter on—it'll be well worth my month of study.

Perhaps that evening after dinner, I'll turn on the TV in my hotel room. And maybe, if I'm lucky, I'll understand one out of every two hundred words. The trick, ultimately, is to not let that discourage me, to think, *Oh well. That's more than I understood the last time I watched TV in Germany*. That was a few years back, in Stuttgart. There was a television mounted on a perch in my room, and I turned it on to find a couple having sex. This wasn't on pay-per-view but just regular Sunday night TV. And I mean these two were really going at it. If I'd had the Lonely Planet guide to German, I might have recognized "Please don't stop!" "That was amazing/ weird." With Herr Thomas, I could understand "I just gave it to you" and, with Pimsleur, "I would like to come now."

I watched this couple for a minute or two, and then I advanced to the next channel, which was snowed out unless you paid for it. *What could they possibly be doing here that they weren't doing for free on the other station?* I asked myself. *Turning each other inside out?*

And isn't that the joy of foreign travel—there's always something to scratch your head over. You don't have to be fluent in order to wonder. Rather, you can sit there with your mouth open, not exactly dumb, just speechless.

Laugh, Kookaburra

I've been to Australia twice so far, but according to my father, I've never actually seen it. He made this observation at the home of my cousin Joan, whom he and I visited just before Christmas one year, and it came on the heels of an equally aggressive comment. "Well," he said, "David's a better *reader* than he is a writer." This from someone who hasn't opened a book since *Dave Stockton's Putt to Win,* in 1996. He's never been to Australia either. Never even come close.

"No matter," he told me. "In order to see the country, you have to see the country*side,* and you've only been to Sydney."

"And Melbourne. And Brisbane," I said. "And I have too gone into the country."

"Like hell you have."

"All right," I said. "Let's get Hugh on the phone. He'll tell you. He'll even send you pictures."

Joan and her family live in Binghamton, New York. They don't see my father and me that often,

so it was pretty lousy to sit at their table, he and I
bickering like an old married couple. Ashamed by the
bad impression we were making, I dropped the countryside business, and as my dad moved on to other
people's shortcomings, I thought back to the previous summer and my daylong flight from London to
Sydney. I was in Australia on business, and because
someone else was paying for the ticket and it would
be possible to stop in Japan on the way home, Hugh
joined me. This is not to put Australia down, but
we'd already gone once before. Then too, spend that
much time on a plane, and you're entitled to a whole
new world when you step off at the other end—the
planet Mercury, say, or at the very least Mexico City.
For an American, though, Australia seems pretty familiar: same wide streets, same office towers. It's
Canada in a thong, or that's the initial impression.

I hate to admit it, but my dad was right about
the countryside. Hugh and I didn't see much of it,
but we wouldn't have seen anything were it not for
a woman named Pat, who was born in Melbourne
and has lived there for most of her life. We'd met
her a few years earlier, in Paris, where she'd come
to spend a mid-July vacation. Over drinks in our living room, her face dewed with sweat, she taught us
the term "shout," as in, "I'm shouting lunch." This
means that you're treating and that you don't want
any lip about it. "You can also say, 'It's my shout,'
or, 'I'll shout the next round,'" she told us.

We kept in touch after her visit, and when my
work was done and I was given a day and a half
to spend as I liked, Pat offered herself as a guide.

On that first afternoon, she showed us around Melbourne and shouted coffee. The following morning she picked us up at our hotel and drove us into what she called "the bush." I expected a wasteland of dust and human bones, but in fact it was nothing like that. When Australians say "the bush," they mean the woods. The forest.

First, though, we had to get out of Melbourne and drive beyond the seemingly endless suburbs. It was August, the dead of winter, and so we had the windows rolled up. The homes we passed were made of wood, many with high fences around the backyards. They didn't look exactly like American houses, but I couldn't quite identify the difference. *Is it the roofs?* I wondered. *The siding?* Pat was driving, and as we passed the turnoff for a shopping center, she invited us to picture a four-burner stove.

"Gas or electric?" Hugh asked, and she said that it didn't matter.

This was not a real stove but a symbolic one, used to prove a point at a management seminar she'd once attended. "One burner represents your family, one is your friends, the third is your health, and the fourth is your work." The gist, she said, was that in order to be successful, you have to cut off one of your burners. And in order to be *really* successful, you have to cut off two.

Pat has her own business, a good one that's allowing her to retire at fifty-five. She owns three houses and two cars, but even without the stuff, she seems like a genuinely happy person. And that alone constitutes success.

I asked which two burners she had cut off, and she said that the first to go had been family. After that she switched off her health. "How about you?"

I thought for a moment and said that I'd cut off my friends. "It's nothing to be proud of, but after meeting Hugh I quit making an effort."

"And what else?" she asked.

"Health, I guess."

Hugh's answer was work.

"And?"

"Just work," he said.

I asked Pat why she'd cut off her family, and with no trace of bitterness, she talked about her parents, both severe alcoholics. They drank away their jobs and credit, and because they were broke, they moved a lot, most often in the middle of the night. This made it hard to have a pet, though for a short time, Pat and her sister managed to own a sheep. It was an old, beat-up ram they named Mr. Preston. "He was lovely and good-natured, until my father sent him off to be shorn," Pat said. "When he returned there were bald patches and horrible, deep cuts, like stab wounds in his skin. Then we moved to an apartment and had to get rid of him." She looked at her hands on the steering wheel. "Poor old Mr. Preston. I hadn't thought about him in years."

It was around this time that we finally entered the bush. Hugh pointed out the window at a still lump of dirty fur lying beside a fallen tree, and Pat caroled, "Roadkill!" Then she pulled over so we could take a closer look. Since leaving Melbourne, we'd been climbing higher into the foothills. The temperature had dropped, and there were graying patches of snow on the ground. I had on a sweater and a jacket, but they weren't quite enough, and I shivered as we walked toward the body and saw that it was a . . . what, exactly? "A teenage kangaroo?"

"A wallaby," Pat corrected me.

The thing had been struck but not run over. It hadn't decomposed or been disfigured, and I was surprised by the shoddiness of its coat. It was as if you'd bred a rabbit with a mule. Then there was the tail, which reminded me of a lance.

"Hugh," I called, "come here and look at the wallaby."

It's his belief that in marveling at a dead animal on the roadside, you may as well have killed it yourself—not accidentally but on purpose, cackling, most likely, as you ran it down. Therefore he stayed in the car.

"It's your loss," I called, and a great cloud of steam issued from my mouth.

Our destination that afternoon was a place called Daylesford, which looked, when we arrived, more like a movie set than an actual working town. The buildings on the main street were two stories tall and made of wood, like buildings in the Old West but brightly painted. Here was the shop selling handmade soaps shaped like petits fours. Here was the fudgery, the jammery, your source for moisturizer. If Dodge City had been founded and maintained by homosexuals, this is what it might have looked like.

"The spas are fantastic," Pat said, and she parked the car in front of a puppet shop. From there we walked down a slight hill, passing a flock of sulfur-crested cockatoos just milling about, pulling worms from the front lawn of a bed-and-breakfast. This was the moment when familiarity slipped away and Australia seemed not just distant, but impossibly foreign. "Will you look at that," I said.

It was Pat who had made the lunch reservation. The restaurant was attached to a hotel, and on arriving we were seated beside a picture window. The view was of a wooden deck and, immediately beyond it, a small lake. On a sunny day it was probably blinding, but the winter sky was like brushed aluminum. The water beneath it had the same dull sheen, and its surface reflected nothing.

Even before the menus were handed out, you could see what sort of a place this was. Order the pork and it might resemble a rough-hewn raft, stranded by tides on a narrow beach of polenta. Fish might come with shredded turnips or a pabulum of coddled fruit. The younger an ingredient, the more highly it was valued, thus the baby chicken, the baby spinach, the newborn asparagus, each pale stalk as slender as a fang.

As always in a fancy restaurant, I asked Hugh to order for me. "Whatever you think," I told him. "Just so long as there's no chocolate in it."

He and Pat weighed our options, and I watched the hostess seat a party of eight. Bringing up the rear was a woman in her midthirties, pretty, and with a baby on her shoulder. Its back was covered with a shawl, but to judge from the size it looked extremely young—a month old, tops.

Keep it away from the chef, I thought.

. A short while later, I noticed that the child hadn't shifted position. Its mother was running her hand over its back, almost as if she were feeling for a switch, and when the top of the shawl fell away, I saw that this was not a baby, but a baby doll.

"*Psssst,*" I whispered, and when Pat raised her eyes, I directed them to the other side of the room.

"Is that normal in Australia?" I asked.

"Maybe it's a grieving thing," she offered. "Maybe she lost a baby in childbirth and this is helping her to work through it."

There's a definite line between looking and staring, and after I was caught crossing it, I turned toward the window. On the highest rail of the deck was a wooden platform, and standing upon it, looking directly into my eyes, was what I knew to be a kookaburra. This thing was as big as a seagull but squatter, squarer, and all done up in earth tones, the complete spectrum from beige to dark walnut. When seen full on, the feathers atop his head looked like brush-cut hair, and that gave him a brutish, almost conservative look. If owls were the professors of the avian kingdom, then kookaburras, I thought, might well be the gym teachers.

When the waitress arrived, I pointed out the window and asked her a half dozen questions, all of them fear-based. "Oh," she said, "that bird's not going to hurt anybody." She took our orders and then she must have spoken to one of the waiters. He was a tall fellow, college age, and he approached our table with a covered bowl in his hands. I assumed it was an appetizer, but it seemed instead that it was for the kookaburra. "Would you like to step outside and feed him?" he asked.

I wanted to say that between the wallaby and the baby doll, I was already overstimulated, but how often in life do you get such an offer? That's how I found myself on the deck, holding a bowl of raw duck meat cut into slender strips. At the sight of it, the bird stood up and flew onto my arm, which buckled slightly beneath his weight.

"Don't be afraid," the waiter said, and he talked to the kookaburra in a soothing, respectful voice, the way you might to a child with a switchblade in his hand. For that's what this thing's beak was—a serious weapon. I held a strip of raw duck, and after yanking it from my fingers, the bird flew back to the railing. Then he took the meat and began slamming it against his wooden platform. *Whap, whap, whap.* Over and over, as if he were tenderizing it.

"This is what he'd do in the wild with snakes and lizards and such," the waiter said. "He thinks it's still alive, see. He thinks he's killing it."

The kookaburra must have slammed the meat against the wooden platform a good ten times. Only then did he swallow it, and look up, expectantly, for more.

I took another strip from the bowl, and the action repeated itself. *Whap, whap, whap.* On or about his third helping, I got used to the feel of a bird on my arm and started thinking about other things, beginning with the word "kookaburra." I first heard it in the fifth grade, when our music teacher went on an Australian kick. She taught us to sing "Waltzing Matilda," "Tie Me Kangaroo Down, Sport," and what we called simply "Kookaburra." I'd never heard such craziness in my life. The first song, for instance, included the words "jumbuck," "billabong," "swagman," and "tuckerbag," none of which were ever explained. The more nonsensical the lyric, the harder it was to remember, and that, most likely, is why I retained the song about the kookaburra—it was less abstract than the others.

I recall that after school that day, I taught it to my sister Amy, who must have been in the first grade at the time. We sang it in the car, we sang it at the table, and then, one night, we sang it in her bed, the two of us lying side by side and rocking back and forth.

We'd been at it for half an hour when the door flung open. "What the hell is going on?" It was our father, one hand resting teapot-style on his hip, and the other—what would be the spout—formed into a fist. He was dressed in his standard around-the-house outfit, which is to say, his underpants. No matter the season he wore them without a shirt or socks, the way a toddler might pad about in a diaper. For as long as any of us could remember, this was the way it went: he returned home from work and stepped out of his slacks, sighing with relief, as if they were oppressive, like high heels. All said, my father looked good in his underpants. Silhouetted in the doorway, he resembled a wrestler. Maybe not one in tip-top condition, but he was closer than any of the other dads on our street. "It's one o'clock in the morning, for God's sake. David, get to your room."

I knew that it was at best ten thirty. Still, though, there was no point in arguing. Down in the basement, I went to my room and he resumed his position in front of the TV. Within a few minutes he was snoring, and I crept back upstairs to join Amy for another twenty rounds.

It didn't take long for our father to rally. "Did I not tell you to go to your room?"

What would strike me afterward was the innocence of it. If I had children and they stayed up late, singing a song about a bird, I believe I would find it charming. *I knew I had those two for a reason,* I think I'd say to myself. I might go so far as to secretly record them and submit the tape in a My Kids Are Cuter Than Yours competition. My dad, by contrast, clearly didn't see it that way, which was strange to me. It's not like we were ruining his TV reception. He couldn't even hear us from that distance, so what did he have to complain about? "All right, sonny, I'm giving you ten seconds. One. Two..."

I guess what he resented was being dismissed. Had our mother told us to shut up, we'd probably have done it. He, on the other hand, sitting around in his underpants—it just didn't seem that important.

At the count of six I pushed back the covers. "I'm going," I spat, and once again I followed my father downstairs.

Ten minutes later, I was back. Amy cleared a space for me, and we picked up where we had left off. "Laugh, Kookaburra! Laugh, Kookaburra! Gay your life must be."

Actually, maybe it was that last bit that bothered him. An eleven-year-old boy in bed with his sister, not just singing about a bird but doing it as best he could, rocking back and forth and imagining himself onstage, possibly wearing a cape and performing before a multitude.

The third time he came into the room, our father was a wild man. Even worse, he was wielding a prop, the dreaded fraternity paddle. It looked like a beaver's tail made out of wood. In my memory, there were Greek letters burned into one side, and crowded around them were the signatures of other Beta Epsilons, men we'd never met, with old-fashioned nicknames like Lefty and Slivers—names, to me, as synonymous with misfortune as Smith & Wesson. Our father didn't bring out the paddle very often, but when he did, he always used it.

"All right, you, let's get this over with." Amy knew that she had nothing to worry about. He was after me, the instigator, so she propped herself against the pillows, drawing up her legs as I scooted to the other side of the bed, then stood there, dancing from foot to foot. It was the worst possible strategy, as evasion only made him angrier. Still, who in his right mind would surrender to such a punishment?

He got me eventually, the first blows landing just beneath my knee caps. Then down I went, and he moved in on my upper thigh. *Whap, whap, whap.* And while it certainly hurt, I have to say that he didn't go overboard. He never did. I asked him about it once, when I was around fourteen, and he chalked it up to a combination of common sense and remarkable self-control. "I know that if I don't stop myself early I'll kill you," he said.

As always after a paddling, I returned to my room vowing never to talk to my father again. To hell with him, to hell with my mother, who'd done nothing to stop him, to hell with Amy for not taking a few licks herself, and to hell with the others, who were, by now, certainly whispering about it.

I didn't have the analogy of the stovetop back then, but what I'd done was turn off the burner marked "family." Then I'd locked my door and sat there simmering, knowing even then that without them, I was nothing. Not a son or a brother but just a boy—and how could that ever be enough? As a full-grown man it seems no different. Cut off your family, and how would you know who you are? Cut them off in order to gain success, and how could that success be measured? What would it possibly mean?

I thought of this as the kookaburra, finally full, swallowed his last strip of duck meat, and took off over the lake. Inside the restaurant, our first courses had arrived, and I watched through the window as Hugh and Pat considered their plates. I should have gone inside right then, but I needed another minute to take it all in and acknowledge, if only to myself, that I really did have it made. A storybook town on the far side of the world, enough in my pocket to shout a fancy lunch, and the sound of that bird in the distant trees, laughing. Laughing.

Standing Still

For a while when I was twenty-three I worked at a restaurant in downtown Raleigh. The place wasn't strictly vegetarian, but it leaned in that direction. "Natural," people called it. My pay wasn't much—three fifty an hour—but lunch was provided and I could occasionally take home leftovers: half-moons of stale pita bread, cups of beige tahini dressing. Lettuce. Twice a week the cook would roast turkeys, and after she had carved off the meat for sandwiches, I was allowed the carcasses, which I would carry back to my apartment and boil for soup. This I would eat with mayonnaise-smeared crackers or maybe an omelet filled with rice.

My average day at the restaurant started at eleven thirty and ended three hours later, earning me, after taxes, around forty dollars a week. My rent was a hundred fifty a month, and in order to pay it, I had to take on other part-time jobs: painting an apartment if I was lucky, or helping out on construction sites—work I got, and very meagerly, through word of mouth. I should have quit the restaurant and found something more substantial, but I told myself I needed the free time, needed it for my *real* work, my sculpture. This wasn't completely unfounded. I'd been in a couple of juried shows, one at the state art museum. For a few hours every day I applied myself. I bundled sticks, I arranged things in cardboard boxes. I typed cryptic notes onto index cards and suspended them from my ceiling.

I could have easily held a full-time job, then come home at night and tied twigs together, but in a way I needed the poverty, needed it as proof that I was truly creative. It was a cliché, of course, but one that was reinforced every time you turned around. People didn't say "artist," they said "starving artist," so even if you weren't doing anything of consequence, as long as you were hungry you were on the right track, weren't you?

Being broke was also an excuse to stay put. When I was twenty there'd been no stopping me. I'd been fearless—the type who'd hitchhike to Mexico on a dare. I lived in San Francisco for a while, and in Oregon. Then I returned to my parents' basement and lost whatever nerve I'd ever had. Since I'd come back to Raleigh, my most daring achievement was to move into my own apartment, this at my father's insistence and done practically at knifepoint. Meaning well, my mother would visit with groceries. "I just thought you could use some meat," she'd say, handing me a blood-soaked bag with ground beef and pork chops and sometimes twenty dollars in it.

My situation improved somewhat in the winter of

1981, when my sister Gretchen moved into the apartment upstairs. Because I was a few years older, she looked up to me; not so much that it strained her neck, but enough to make me feel that I wasn't completely worthless. When I saw myself through my parents' eyes, I saw a worm crawling through mud and shit toward a psychedelic mushroom, but when I saw myself through hers, I felt that things were possibly not as bad as they seemed. I wasn't broken, just resting, readying myself for the next big thing.

Gretchen had just completed two and a half years of college in the mountains of North Carolina, at the same school I had gone to for a while. Now she was hoping to transfer to the Rhode Island School of Design, promising that if she got in, she'd never refer to it as "Risdee."

"We'll see about that," I said, knowing that when a person gets busy, the first things to go are the extra syllables.

Gretchen submitted her portfolio, and while waiting to see if she'd been accepted, she enrolled in an entomology class at NC State and took a waitressing job at a pizza parlor near the university. At the end of every shift she'd collect a couple of leftover slices, some with the mushrooms or pepperoni picked off, and bring them to me wrapped in foil. Then I'd get high and she'd trot out her insects, one of which was usually languishing in her killing jar. This she carried everywhere she went, a portable gas chamber for any lacewing, caddis fly, or camel cricket unfortunate enough to catch her attention.

As spring arrived and her death toll mounted, I

found extra work at the university, modeling for a life-drawing class. I didn't do it nude, or even shirtless—I was far too modest—and for that reason I was called in only occasionally. Because I was clothed, the instructor, a woman named Susan, encouraged me to arrive with a variety of outfits, the more conflicting prints the better. "And don't forget hats!" she said.

When frozen stock-still before a roomful of students, I'd find that my thoughts usually drifted toward money, one instance in particular when I had it in my grasp and foolishly let it slip away. That had happened shortly after the New Year, when I'd gone with a friend to the Hirshhorn Museum in Washington, DC. Before setting out to see the collection, we left our things with the woman at the coat check. When it came time to leave, I presented this same woman with my stub, and after searching around in her racks, she returned to hand me a full-length mink, auburn-colored and lined with emerald green satin. It was much heavier than I'd expected, like holding a bear that had fainted in my arms. After thinking it might be a trick, I realized that the woman wasn't paying attention. All the easier, then, to turn around and walk out the door. I was close enough to feel the cold air on my face when I chickened out and returned to the coat check. "I'm sorry," I said, "but you seem to have made a mistake."

The woman looked at the mink laid before her on the counter. "And you're just *now* noticing it?" she asked.

"What a bitch," I said to my friend, walking to

the car in my thrift-store overcoat. "She should have been thanking me. Better still, she should have *rewarded* me."

How stupid can you get? I now thought, standing before a classroom with a paisley turban on my head. *That mink could have made a real difference in my life.* It wasn't exactly stealing, I reasoned, not technically. The coat's rightful owner would have been compensated, so who, really, would it have harmed?

The building that Gretchen and I lived in—a large shabby house now sliced into apartments—was located midway between downtown and the university. Neither of us knew how to drive, so when going to work or school, we either walked, cycled, or begged people for rides, just like we had when we were children. Half a mile away, on the other side of a fine, well-manicured neighborhood, there was a shopping center called Cameron Village. It included a twenty-four-hour supermarket, and while walking home from it one night, a bag of groceries in one hand and her killing jar in the other, my sister was attacked by a man who came from behind and tried to drag her into the bushes.

He had the element of surprise, but Gretchen's tall, at least for a Sedaris, and powerful. As soon as she got her bearings, she broke loose and headed to the nearest house for help. No lights came on, so she ran three blocks down the middle of the street and onto our front porch. I heard a banging on my door, and when I opened it she bolted past me into the kitchen, then stood trembling and mute—in shock, most likely, and with leaves in her hair. I phoned the police and set about hiding my drugs. After that I called my parents, aware that I was stealing someone else's news, and aware too of how dramatic I sounded. "Gretchen's been attacked."

The officer who arrived began by saying that he'd been in my apartment once before. "It was a narcotics case, years ago," he told me, looking from the kitchen to the living room, where dozens of index cards dangled from the ceiling. He took my sister's statement, and as he drove off to canvass the area, our parents pulled up, my mother saying before she'd even set her purse down that this was all Gretchen's fault. "Walking to the store at eleven o'clock at night, you were as good as asking for it!"

Our father, who has always distorted time to suit his purposes, put the blame on me. "It was one o'clock in the morning, and you let your sister wander the streets by herself?"

"It wasn't one," I said. "It's not even one now."

"Aw, baloney."

The policeman returned carrying Gretchen's grocery bag along with a mayonnaise jar containing a half-dead moth and a ball of cotton soaked in fingernail polish remover. "Is this...yours?" he asked.

My father gave my sister his "now I've seen it all" look. "Oh, that's nice," he said. "Caught yourself a pretty little butterfly while you were traipsing home alone at two in the morning?"

*   *   *

The following day he took Gretchen to the police station, where she was scheduled to look through mug shots. The fellow who'd attacked her had been black. She'd noticed he was wearing a white T-shirt, but then her glasses got knocked off and it all became a blur.

"All right," said the policeman. "Let's talk about pants. Think now—were they long or short?"

When Gretchen said "long," my father slapped his palm on the tabletop. "There you go," he said. "*Now* we're getting somewhere!"

After that day's shift at the natural-foods restaurant, I returned to my apartment and found my dad and sister waiting for me. "We can't count on the police to catch this guy," my father said. "So what we're going to do is ride around and see if we can't find him ourselves."

"We're going to drive around and look for a black man?" I asked.

"With long pants and a white T-shirt on," Gretchen added. "Clothes he couldn't possibly have changed because they're permanently attached to his body."

"Don't be a smart-ass," our father said. "This person tried to rape you, don't forget. You think it's just a onetime thing, like, 'Well, that didn't work, so I guess I'll turn my life around, maybe sell ice cream instead'?"

He wasn't the only one who was angry. All morning at work I'd imagined myself going back in time and coming across this person as he attacked my sister. In the fantasy I was just walking along, minding my own business at eleven o'clock on a Wednesday night, when I heard a woman scream and saw some movement in the bushes. At this, I grabbed the guy by the collar, saying something polite but at the same time hostile, like, "Excuse me, friend..." Then I imagined hitting him the way men in movies did, my fist making contact with a smart cracking sound, his jaw splitting open like a ripe melon. Once I got him down on the ground, I'd pound on him until Gretchen jumped in, saying, "David, stop! Stop before you kill him."

It was an engaging little daydream but would have been a lot more satisfying if the guy had been white, or at least whit*ish*, a Spanish exchange student, or a traveling Hawaiian in town on business. Of all the possibilities, why did he have to be black, especially in North Carolina, where everything was so loaded? I think Gretchen was feeling the same way—not that she needed to let this slide but that she was caught up in some tiresome cliché. Now here was her father organizing a posse.

The situation got weirder still when I noticed the baseball bat lying across the backseat of the car. This wasn't something that had been brought from home—we'd no sooner own a baseball bat than a trident. Rather, it was brand-new and still had a price tag on it.

"You *bought* a baseball bat?"

"Calm down," my father told me. "If we don't catch the guy, maybe your brother can use it."

"For what?" I said. "Since when does Paul care about baseball? On top of that, you don't even know who we're looking for."

My father was hoping that Gretchen might identify her attacker through his body language—the way he walked or moved his hands. Likelier still, she could perhaps recognize his voice. This was possible, surely, and I could understand it if the field of potential suspects was narrowed down—a lineup of five behind mirrored glass, say. As it stood, every black male in Raleigh between the ages of eighteen and sixty-five was a possible candidate, especially those with long pants and white T-shirts on.

"This is ridiculous," Gretchen moaned. Our father drove past the pancake house and turned onto Hillsborough Street, stopping soon after to point to a black man. "Does that one look familiar?" he asked.

The guy was perhaps in his early twenties and was holding a can of Coke to his mouth, a can he lowered when we pulled alongside him and my father stuck his head out the window. "Listen," he said, "I need you to tell me how to get to the Capitol Building."

The young man pointed in the direction we had come from and said that it wasn't very far.

My father turned to Gretchen. "Is anything coming back to you?"

"Dad, please."

Sensing something strange was happening, the young man stepped away from the car and continued down the street. "Hey," my father called. "Hey, you!"

The next black man he stopped had a beat-up cast on his arm, and the one after that had an African accent and scars like whiskers on his face. Then Gretchen asked to be taken back to her apartment.

She was waitressing that night, and my father insisted on driving her to work. Getting her home, he let me know, was *my* responsibility. "I still can't believe you let her wander around by herself at three o'clock in the morning."

One thing the adults all seemed to agree on was that Gretchen was remiss in walking to the grocery store. So remiss, according to some, that you couldn't really blame the guy who attacked her, as what was he *supposed* to think, a young woman out on her own at that hour—a young woman in shorts, no less?

"But doesn't the killing jar count for anything?" I argued. "Is it that hard to distinguish a prostitute from a college student? Whores don't wear glasses. And what about me? I walk to the store all the time."

The rules, of course, were different for women. When they were young, each of my sisters was approached by a stranger, someone in a car who'd pretend to be lost and needing directions. The girls would come up to the rolled-down window and see that the driver's pants were unzipped, that his penis was hard, and that he was stroking it. It wasn't the same guy every time—one might be bald and wearing sunglasses, while another could have long sideburns and a lazy eye—but it happened in turn to all the Sedaris girls. They'd see a man their father's age masturbating, and afterward they'd wander into the house, never hysterical but slightly dazed, as if they'd been stopped by a talking cat.

I felt left out and remember asking my father why it never happened to me.

"Well, think about it," he said. "Exposing yourself to a girl is one thing. Doing it to a boy, though—the guy would have to be perverted."

Then there were the strangers who called the house. "You want to eat my *what?*" I once heard my mother say into the receiver. "Buddy, if that's what you're after, you are talking to the wrong lady." Then she laughed, not cruelly but in a way that seemed genuine. Had she said, "Here, let me put my daughter on the phone," it wouldn't have surprised me.

There'd been something almost comic about the exhibitionists and crank callers, the sense that, more than anything, these men were to be pitied. Touching, though, that was something else. Then there was the racial divide. I don't mean to suggest that my father was operating on a double standard—he'd have gone out looking for a white would-be rapist as well. I just don't think he'd have felt so frustrated and out of his element.

The day after poring over mug shots, Gretchen had a class. I worked at the restaurant and came home to find my dad sitting on my front porch. It seemed that, with my sister or without her, he was determined to find the man who'd attacked her. It was beyond ridiculous at this point, but I think he knew that. Someone you love is assaulted by a stranger, and you can either sit at home and do nothing or drive around with an iced vodka and water tinkling between your legs, not just looking at other men but *really* looking at them, studying them, the way the students in the drawing class studied me. "Well, *that's* something new," my father said at one point, gesturing to a guy with a shower cap on his head.

It was rare for my dad and me to spend time alone, rarer still to be on the same team, and with a bat, no less. We both wanted to protect Gretchen, though neither of us was ultimately able to. After getting accepted to RISD, she moved to Providence and even learned to drive. She was in her car one night and had just pulled up in front of her apartment when a man yanked open the passenger door and jumped in beside her. "He was white," she reported, "wearing jeans and a red plaid jacket." Luckily she scared him off by laying on her horn. A few months later, following a long shift at the restaurant she worked at, she fell asleep and awoke to find three men standing around her bed. This was a case of her needing protection from herself, as it turned out they were firefighters. It seemed she'd gone to bed with a pan of popcorn on the stove and had slept through the kitchen full of smoke, the phone calls from her neighbors, and the concerted pounding on her door.

All that was in the future on the afternoon my father and I cruised around Raleigh, looking for potential rapists. For a while the two of us talked about Gretchen, imagining the worst that might have happened and stoking our anger. Then we talked about all my sisters and how much they needed us, or at least him. I was disappointed when my dad's drink ran out and he headed back to drop me off at my apartment. I somehow hadn't realized until that moment how much I dreaded the place, how freighted it was with the sense of failure. It seemed that I'd missed some pivotal step on the path to adulthood. My father went from high school to the navy to college to IBM, skipping from one to the next like they were stones in a river he was crossing. These wouldn't have been my choices, surely, but you had to admire his single-mindedness. When I thought of my path, I recalled several quaaludes I'd taken a week earlier, pills that had somehow caused me to fall up the flight of stairs from my apartment to Gretchen's. Was this what the rest of my life would be like? I wanted to say to my father, "Help me," but what came out was "Do you think you could maybe loan me twenty dollars?"

"There is absolutely no chance of that happening," he said.

"What about ten?"

It wasn't long afterward that Gretchen got her acceptance letter. The news superseded her attack, and though she wouldn't move for another three months, in a way it was like she'd already gone. The incident that had bound us together now felt like the end of something, a chapter that for her might be titled "The Life Before My Real Life Began."

I missed the pizza after she'd left, but more than that I missed her, missed having someone naive enough to believe in me. When she returned she'd be just like the other friends who'd moved on, the ones who flew home for Christmas and made you feel like a loser. Not that they tried to. Sure, they'd mention their celebrity sightings, the art shows and opportunities in their exciting new cities, but always there would come that moment when their talk turned back to Raleigh and how much they supposedly missed it. "Because the people, my God," they'd say. "And you can get such good spaces here—an apartment for, what do you pay, David, one fifty a month?"

A person needed savings in order to move, but more than that he needed gumption. The mink I'd returned that day in Washington would not have helped me get out of North Carolina. With the money I could have sold it for, I'd have undoubtedly stayed just where I was, living meagerly from week to week and inventing other excuses for myself. It did not escape my attention that while modeling for the drawing class I was both literally and figuratively standing still. It was a position I'd hold for another three years, a long time when you're going nowhere, and an interminable one when you're going nowhere fast.

Just a Quick E-mail

Hey, Robin,

Just a quick e-mail to thank you for the wedding gift, or "wedding gift *certificate*," I guess I should say. Two free pizzas—how thoughtful of you. And how generous: any toppings we want!

Maybe you hadn't heard that I'd registered at Tumbridge & Colchester. Last June, I think it was, just before we announced the engagement. Not that the pizzas didn't come in handy; they did, though in a slightly indirect way. Unlike you, who're so wonderfully unconcerned with what other people think, I'm a bit vain, especially when it comes to my figure. That being the case, I used the certificates to feed our workmen, who are currently building a small addition. I know you thought our house was big enough already. "Tara meets DressBarn" was how I heard you so cleverly describe it at the wedding. "I mean, really," you said. "How much room do two people need?"

Or did you say, "Two *thin* people"? What with the

band playing and everyone in the world shouting their congratulations, it was a little hard to hear. Just like it is at our ever-expanding house—the workers all hammering away! What they've done is tear down the wall between the kitchen and the breakfast nook. That'll give us room for a walk-in silverware drawer and this new sixteen-burner stove I've been eyeing. Plus it will allow us to expand the counter space, put in a second dishwasher, and install an electric millstone for grinding blue corn. (Homemade tortillas, anyone?) Then we're going to enclose that useless deck, insulate it, and create a separate dining room for when we go Asian. This will eliminate that ramp you're so fond of, but it's not like we see you all that often and I don't think it will kill you to crawl up a half dozen stairs. As a matter of fact, as long as they're clean, I actually think it might be good for you.

Seeing as we're on this subject, Robin, is it right to insist on all this special treatment? More than that, is it *healthy?* It's been almost a year since the car accident. Don't you think it's time you moved on with your life? Do I need to remind you of all *my* injuries: the dislocated shoulder, the practically broken wrist that still tingles when I do something strenuous like whisk in damp weather? On top of that, it took me days to wash your blood out of my hair. The admitting nurse put me down as a redhead—that's how bad it was—your left front tooth practically embedded in my skull! It's no severed spinal cord, of course, but like Dr. Gaffney says, the ball is in *your* court now. Either you can live in the past as a lonely, bitter paraplegic, or you can live in the present as one. I dusted myself off and got back on the proverbial horse, so why can't you?

In other news, did you get the postcard I sent from our honeymoon? Iraq was beautiful, just as I imagined it would be, but there were *so many* Americans there! I said to Philip, "Is nowhere safe? I mean, really. In terms of the crowds, we might as well have gone to Paris!" Then, of course, we *did* go to Paris, but it was for work rather than vacation. Philip had a client he needed to meet, an American in town for some big Chablis auction. He once defended her on a drunk-driving charge, and successfully too, this despite her Breathalyzer results and some pretty bad behavior, some of which was caught on video. Now they're suing the people she hit, or at least the one who lived, and it looks like they've got a fairly good chance of winning. This is not to worry you in any way. What with the addition on the house and the million and a half other things on my to-do list, a lawsuit is the last thing on my mind. Not that it wasn't proposed.

While my hardworking husband consulted with his client, I, alone, wandered the quays, stopping every now and then to duck into a boutique. And more than once I thought of you. For Paris, I remembered, is where *you* and Philip honeymooned. That was in the good old days, when the dollar and the euro were practically even. Now it costs a king's ransom just for a cup of coffee and a croque-madame, so a pair of shoes from Christian Louboutin—well, you can just imagine! I suppose that for you it would make sense, but for someone who walks the way I do, someone known to practically gallop when there's a sale taking place—the shoes I got are good for one, maybe two seasons at the most. Still, though, what could I do? Iraq had been totally picked over by the time we arrived, and I wanted a little something to remind me of my trip.

After returning stateside Philip went right to work. His number one job: to make me happy. First, we started on the addition ($$$$$$$), then came a successful effort to erase that DWI from my driving record. It wasn't easy, but legal matters rarely are. All I can say is that if it helps to have friends, it helps even more to have friends who are governors!

None of this will get you out of your wheelchair, but it *will* restore my self-confidence and what I like to think of as my good name. It means, as well, that you'll have to stop calling me the "drunken bitch" who "took away" your legs and then "stole" your husband. "Drunk," it seems, is a relative term, and if I were you I'd watch how I used it. The leg bit is an exaggeration, as you clearly still *have* them (big purple veins and all). As for the stealing, Philip came to me of his own volition—one adult to another, no coercion involved. In the end all you're left with is the single word "bitch," which could mean any number of things. I myself would use it to describe someone whose idea of an appropriate wedding present is a gift certificate for two pizzas! Offering it to your ex-husband, I can understand, but to your own sister? That's just tacky.

Gotta run!
—Ronda

A Guy Walks into a Bar Car

In the golden age of American travel, the platforms of train stations were knee-deep in what looked like fog. You see it all the time in black-and-white movies, these low-lying eddies of silver. I always thought it was steam from the engines, but now I wonder if it didn't come from cigarettes. You could smoke everywhere back then: in the dining car, in your sleeping berth. Depending on your preference, it was either absolute heaven or absolute hell.

I know there was a smoking car on the Amtrak I took from Raleigh to Chicago in 1984, but seven years later it was gone. By then if you wanted a cigarette, your only option was to head for the bar. It sounds all right in passing, romantic even—"the bar on the Lake Shore Limited"—but in fact it was rather depressing. Too bright, too loud, and full of alcoholics who commandeered the seats immediately after boarding and remained there, marinating like cheap kebabs, until they reached their destinations. At first their voices might strike you as jolly: the warm tones of strangers becoming friends. Then the drinkers would get sloppy and repetitive, settling, finally, on that cross-eyed mush that passes for alcoholic sincerity.

On the train I took from New York to Chicago in early January 1991, one of the drunks pulled down his pants and shook his bare bottom at the woman behind the bar. I was thirty-four, old enough to know better, yet I laughed along with everyone else. The trip was interminable—almost nineteen hours, not counting any delays—but nothing short of a derailment could have soured my good mood. I was off to see the boyfriend I'd left behind when I moved to New York. We'd known each other for six years, and though we'd broken up more times than either of us could count, there was the hope that this visit might reunite us. Then he'd join me for a fresh start in Manhattan, and all our problems would disappear.

It was best for both of us that it didn't work out that way, though of course I couldn't see it at the time. The trip designed to bring us back together tore us apart for good, and it was a considerably sorrier me that boarded the Limited back to New York. My train left Union Station in the early evening. The late-January sky was the color of pewter, and the ground beneath it—as flat as rolled-out dough—was glazed with slush. I watched as the city receded into the distance, and then I went to the bar car for a cigarette. Of the dozen or so drunks who'd staggered on board in Chicago, one in particular stood out. I've always had an eye for ruined-looking men, and that's what attracted me to this guy—I'll call him Johnny

Ryan—the sense that he'd been kicked around. Once he hit thirty, a hardness would likely settle about his mouth and eyes, but as it was—at twenty-nine—he was right on the edge, a screw-top bottle of wine the day before it turns to vinegar.

It must have been he who started the conversation, as I'd never have had the nerve. Under different circumstances I might have stammered hello and run back to my seat, but my breakup convinced me that something major was about to happen. The chance of a lifetime was coming my way, and in order to accept it I needed to loosen up, to stop being so "rigid." That was what my former boyfriend had called me. He'd thrown in "judgmental" while he was at it, another of those synonyms for "no fun at all." The fact that it stung reaffirmed what I had always suspected: It was all true. No one was duller, more prudish and set in his ways, than I was.

Johnny didn't strike me as gay, but it was hard to tell with alcoholics. Like prisoners and shepherds, many of them didn't care who they had sex with, the idea being that what happens in the dark stays in the dark. It's the next morning you have to worry about—the name-calling, the slamming of doors, the charge that you somehow cast a spell. I must have been desperate to think that such a person would lead me to a new life. Not that Johnny was bad company—it's just that the things we had in common were all so depressing. Unemployment, for instance. My last job had been as an elf at Macy's.

"Personal assistant" was how I phrased it, hoping he wouldn't ask for whom.

"Uh—Santa?"

His last job had involved hazardous chemicals. An accident at Thanksgiving had caused boils to rise on his back. A few months before that, a tankard of spilled benzene had burned all the hair off his arms and hands. This only made him more attractive. I imagined those smooth pink mitts of his opening the door to the rest of my life.

"So are you just going to stand here smoking all night?" he asked.

Normally I waited until nine o'clock to start drinking, but "What the heck," I said. "I'll have a beer. Why not?" When a couple of seats opened up, Johnny and I took them. Across the narrow carriage a black man with a bushy mustache pounded on his Formica tabletop. "So a nun goes into town," he said, "and sees a sign reading, 'Quickies—twenty-five dollars.' Not sure what it means, she walks back to the convent and pulls aside the mother superior. 'Excuse me,' she asks, 'but what's a quickie?'

"And the old lady goes, 'Twenty-five dollars. Just like in town.'"

As the room filled with laughter, Johnny lit a fresh cigarette. "Some comedian," he said. I don't know how we got onto the subject of gambling—perhaps I asked if he had a hobby.

"I'll bet on sporting events, on horses and grey-hounds—hell, put two fleas on the table and I'll bet over which one can jump the highest. How about you?"

Gambling to me is what a telephone pole might be to a groundhog. He sees that it's there but doesn't for the life of him understand why. Friends have tried to explain the appeal, but still I don't get it. Why take chances with money?

Johnny had gone to Gamblers Anonymous, but the whining got on his nerves and he quit after his third meeting. Now he was on his way to Atlantic City, where he hoped to clean up at the craps table.

"All right," called the black man on the other side of the carriage. "I've got another one: What do you have if you have nuts on a wall?" He lit a cigarette and blew out the match. "Walnuts!"

A red-nosed woman in a decorative sweatshirt started talking, but the black fellow told her that he wasn't done yet. "What do you have if you have nuts on your chest?" He waited a beat. "Chestnuts! What do you have when you have nuts on your chin?" He looked from face to face. "A dick in your mouth!"

"Now that's good," Johnny said. "I'll have to remember that."

"I'll have to remind you," I told him, trembling a little at my forwardness. "I mean...I'm pretty good at holding on to jokes."

As the black man settled down, I asked Johnny about his family. It didn't surprise me that his mother and father were divorced. Each of them was fifty-four years old, and each was currently living with someone much younger. "My dad's girl-friend—fiancée, I guess I should call her—is no older than me," Johnny said. "Before losing my job I had my own place, but now I'm living with them. Just, you know, until I get back on my feet."

I nodded.

"My mom, meanwhile, is a total mess," he said. "Total pothead, total motormouth, total perfect match for her asshole thirty-year-old boyfriend."

Nothing in this guy's life sounded normal to me. Take food: He could recall his mother rolling joints on the kitchen counter, but he couldn't remember her cooking a single meal, not even on holidays. For dinner they'd eat take-out hamburgers or pizzas, sometimes a sandwich slapped together over the sink. Johnny didn't cook either. Neither did his father or future stepmother. I asked what was in their refrigerator, and he said, "Ketchup, beer, mixers—what else?" He had no problem referring to himself as an alcoholic. "It's just a fact," he said. "I have blue eyes and black hair too. Big deal."

"Here's a clean one," the black man said. "A fried-egg sandwich walks into a bar and orders a drink. The bartender looks him up and down, then goes, 'Sorry, we don't serve food here.'"

"Oh, that's old," one of his fellow drunks said. "Not only that, but it's supposed to be a hamburger, not a fried-egg sandwich."

"It's supposed to be *food,* is what it's supposed to be," the black man told him. "As to what that food is, I'll make it whatever the hell I want to."

"Amen," Johnny said, and the black man gave him a thumbs-up.

His next joke went over much better. "What did the leper say to the prostitute? 'Keep the tip.'"

I pictured what looked like a mushroom cap resting in the palm of an outstretched hand. Then I covered my mouth and laughed so hard that beer trickled out of my nose. I was just mopping it up when the last call was announced, and everyone raced to the counter to stock up. Some of the drinkers would be at it until morning when the bar reopened, while others would find their assigned seats and sleep for a while before returning.

As for Johnny, he had a fifth of Smirnoff in his suitcase. I had two Valiums in mine, and, because of my ugly past history with sedatives, the decision to share them came easily. An hour later, it was agreed that we needed to smoke some pot. Each of us was holding, so the only question was where to smoke it—and how to get there from the bar. Since taking the Valium, drinking six beers, and following them with straight vodka, walking had become a problem for me. I don't know what it took to bring down Johnny, but he wasn't even close yet. That's what comes with years of socking it away—you should be unconscious, but instead you're up, and full of bright ideas. "I think I've got a place we can go to," he said.

I'm not sure why he chose the women's lounge rather than the men's. Perhaps it was closer or maybe there was no men's lounge. One way or the other, even now, all these many years later, it shames me to think of it. The idea of holing up in a bathroom, of hogging the whole thing just so that you can hang out with someone who will never, under any circumstances, return your interest, makes me cringe. Especially given that this—the "dressing room," it was called—was Amtrak's one meager attempt to recapture some glamour. It amounted to a small chamber with a window—a space not much bigger than a closet. There was an area to sit while brushing your hair or applying makeup, and a mirror to look into while you did it. A second, inner door led to a sink and toilet, but we kept that shut and installed ourselves on the carpeted floor.

Johnny had brought our plastic cups from the bar, and after settling in, he poured us each a drink. I felt boneless, as if I'd been filleted; yet still I managed to load the pipe and hold my lighter to the bowl. Looking up through the window, I could see the moon, which struck me, in my half-conscious state, as flat and unnaturally bright, a sort of glowing Pringle.

"Do you think we can turn that overhead light off?" I asked.

"No problem, Chief."

It was he who brought up the subject of sex. One moment I was asking if his mom gave him a discount on his drugs, and the next thing I knew he was telling me about this woman he'd recently slept with. "A fatty," he called her. "A bloodsucker." Johnny also told me that the older he got, the harder it was to get it up. "I'll be totally into it and then it's like, 'What the fuck?' You know?"

"Oh, definitely," I said.

He poured more vodka into his plastic cup and swirled it around, as if it were a fine cognac that needed to breathe. "You get into a lot of fights?" he asked.

"Arguments?"

"No," he said. "I mean with your fists. You ever punch people?"

I relit the pipe and thought of the dustup my former boyfriend and I had had before I left. It was the first time since the fifth grade that I'd hit someone not directly related to me, and it left me feeling like a Grade A moron. This had a lot to do with my punch, which was actually more of a slap. To make it worse, I'd then slipped on the icy sidewalk and fallen into a bank of soft gray snow.

There was no need to answer Johnny's fistfight question. The subject had been raised for his benefit rather than mine, an excuse to bemoan the circumference of his biceps. Back when he was boxing, the one on the right had measured seventeen and a half inches. "Now it's less than fourteen," he told me. "I'm shrinking before my very fucking eyes."

"Well, can't you fatten it back up somehow?" I asked. "You're young. I mean, just how hard can it be to gain weight?"

"The problem isn't gaining weight, it's gaining it in the right place," Johnny said. "Two six-packs a day might swell my stomach, but it's not doing shit for my arms."

"Maybe you could lift the cans for a while before opening them," I offered. "That should count for something, shouldn't it?"

Johnny flattened his voice. "You're a regular comedian, aren't you? Keep it up and maybe you can open for that asshole in the bar." A minute of silence and then he relit the pipe, took a hit, and passed it my way. "Look at us," he said, and he let out a long sigh. "A couple of first-class fucking losers."

I wanted to defend myself, to at least point out that we were in *second* class, but then somebody knocked on the door. "Go away," Johnny said. "The bathroom's closed until tomorrow." A minute later there came another knock, this one harder, and before we could respond a key turned and a security guard entered. It wouldn't have worked to deny anything: the room stunk of pot and cigarette smoke. There was the half-empty bottle of vodka, the plastic cups turned on their sides. Put a couple of lamp shades on our heads, and the picture would have been complete.

I suppose the guard could have made some trouble—confiscated our dope, had us arrested at the next stop—but instead he just told us to take a hike, no easy feat on a train. Johnny and I parted without saying good night, I staggering off to my assigned seat, and he going, I assumed, to his. I saw him again the following morning, back in the bar car. Whatever spell had been cast the night before was broken, and he was just another alcoholic starting his day with a shot and a chaser. As I ordered a coffee, the black man told a joke about a witch with one breast.

"Give it a rest," the woman in the decorative sweatshirt said.

I smoked a few cigarettes and then returned to my seat, nursing what promised to be a two-day headache. While slumped against the window, trying unsuccessfully to sleep, I thought of a trip to Greece I'd taken in August 1982. I was twenty-five that summer and flew by myself from Raleigh to Athens. A few days after arriving, I was joined by my father, my brother, and my sister Lisa. The four of us traveled around the country, and when they went back to North Carolina I took a bus to the port city of Patras. From there I sailed to Brindisi, Italy, wondering all the while why I hadn't returned with the rest of my family. In theory it was wonderful—a European adventure. I was too self-conscious to enjoy it, though, too timid, and it stymied me that I couldn't speak the language.

A bilingual stranger helped me buy a train ticket to Rome, but on the return to Brindisi I had no one but myself to rely on. The man behind the counter offered me three options, and I guess I said yes to the one that meant "No seat for me, thank you. I would like to be packed as tightly as possible alongside people with no access to soap or running water."

It was a common request, at least among the young and foreign. I heard French, Spanish, German, and a good many languages I couldn't quite identify. What was it that sounded like English played backward? Dutch? Swedish? If I found the crowd intimidating, it had more to do with my insecurity than with the way anyone treated me. I suppose the others seemed more deserving than I did, with their faded bandannas and goatskin bags sagging with wine. While I was counting the days until I could go back home, they seemed to have a real talent for living.

When I was a young man my hair was dark brown and a lot thicker than it is now. I had one continuous eyebrow instead of two separate ones, and this made me look as though I sometimes rode a donkey. It sounds odd to say it—conceited, even—but I was cute that August when I was twenty-five. I wouldn't have said so at the time, but reviewing pictures taken by my father in Athens, I think, *That was me? Really?* Looks-wise, I feel that single month constituted my moment, a peak from which the descent has been both swift and merciless.

It's only three hundred and fifty miles from Rome to Brindisi, but, what with the constant stopping and starting, the train took forever. We left, I believe, at around eight thirty p.m., and for the first few hours, everyone stood. Then we sat with our legs crossed, folding them in a little bit tighter when one person, and then another, decided to lie down. As my fellow passengers shifted position, I found myself pushed toward the corner, where I brushed up against a fellow named Bashir.

Lebanese, he said he was, en route to a small Italian university, where he planned to get a master's in engineering. Bashir's English was excellent, and in a matter of minutes we formed what passes between wayfarers in a foreign country as a kind of automatic friendship. More than a friendship, actually—a romance. Coloring everything was this train, its steady rumble as we passed through the dark Italian countryside. Bashir was—how to describe him? It was as if you had coaxed the eyes out of Bambi and resettled them, half asleep, into a human face. Nothing hard or ruined-looking there; in fact it was just the opposite—angelic, you might call him, pretty.

What was it that he and I talked about so intently? Perhaps the thrill was that we *could* talk, that our tongues, each flabby from lack of exercise, could flap and make sounds in their old familiar way. Three hours into our conversation, he invited me to get off the train in his college town and spend some time, as much as I liked, in the apartment that was waiting for him. It wasn't the offer you'd make to a backpacker but something closer to a proposal. "Be with me" was the way I interpreted it.

At the end of our train car was a little room, no more than a broom closet, really, with a barred window in it. It must have been four a.m. when two disheveled Germans stepped out, and we moved in to take their place. As would later happen with Johnny Ryan, Bashir and I sat on the floor, the state of which clearly disgusted him. Apart from the fact that we were sober, and were pressed so close that our shoulders touched, the biggest difference was that our attraction was mutual. The moment came when we should have kissed—you could practically hear the surging strings—but I was too shy to make the first move, and so, I guess, was he. Still I could feel this thing between us, not just lust but a kind of immediate love, the sort that, like instant oatmeal, can be realized in a matter of minutes and is just as nutritious as the real thing. *We'll kiss...now*, I kept thinking. Then, *Okay...now*. And on it went, more torturous by the second.

The sun was rising as we reached his destination,

the houses and church spires of this strange city—a city I could make my own—silhouetted against the weak morning sky. "And so?" he asked.

I don't remember my excuse, but it all came down to cowardice. For what, really, did I have to return to? A job pushing a wheelbarrow on Raleigh construction sites? A dumpy one-bedroom next to the IHOP?

Bashir got off with his three big suitcases and became a perennial lump in my throat, one that rises whenever I hear the word "Lebanon" or see its jittery outline on the evening news. *Is that where you went back to?* I wonder. *Do I ever cross your mind? Are you even still alive?*

Given the short amount of time we spent together, it's silly how often, and how tenderly, I think of him. All the way to Penn Station, hungover from my night with Johnny Ryan, I wondered what might have happened had I taken Bashir up on his offer. I imagined our apartment overlooking a square: the burbling fountain, the drawings of dams and bridges piled neatly on the desk.

When you're young it's easy to believe that such an opportunity will come again, maybe even a better one. Instead of a Lebanese guy in Italy it might be a Nigerian one in Belgium, or maybe a Pole in Turkey. You tell yourself that if you traveled alone to Europe this summer, you could surely do the same thing next year, and the year after that. Of course you don't, though, and the next thing you know you're an aging, unemployed elf so desperate for love you spend your evening mooning over a straight alcoholic.

The closer we got to New York, the more miserable I became. Then I thought of this guy my friend Lily and I had borrowed a ladder from a few months earlier, someone named Hugh. I'd never really trusted people who went directly from one relationship to the next, so after my train pulled into Penn Station, and after I'd taken the subway home, I'd wait a few hours, or maybe even a full day, before dialing his number and asking if he'd like to hear a joke.

Author, Author

If anything should be bracketed by matching book-
ends, I suppose it's an author tour. The ones I'd
undertaken in the past had begun in one independent
or chain store, and ended, a month or so later, in
another. The landscape, though, has changed since
then, and it's telling that on my '08 tour I started and
finished at a Costco.

The first one I went to was in Winston-Salem,
North Carolina. I was spending the weekend with
my sister Lisa, gearing up for six weeks of travel,
when her husband, Bob, expressed a need for lightbulbs. "Anyone game for a quick ride to Costco?" he
asked, and before he could even find his keys I was
panting, doglike, beside the front door.

Living in cities, it's easy to avoid the big-box
superstores. Their merciless lighting, their stench
of rubber and cheap molded plastic—it's not the
way I normally like to shop. At Costco, though,
I'd found these displays of pain relievers: Anacin,
Bayer, Tylenol—eight major brands were represent-

ed. Pills were paired into single-serving envelopes, then stapled in rows to a bright sheet of poster board. It looked like something you'd see behind the counter at a gas station. There the packets might cost two dollars each, but here the entire display—maybe a hundred and fifty doses—went for just twelve bucks.

At home I'd buy a bottle of Bufferin or ibuprofen and leave it at that, but when I'm on tour it's packets I need—not for myself but to give as gifts to the people who've come to see me. Say it's someone's birthday or anniversary: I always offer the shampoos and conditioners taken from my hotels. But they provide only so many, and with a good-size crowd you're empty-handed before you know it.

Adults get something for special occasions, but the bulk of my presents go to teenagers, who qualify by virtue of their very existence. Real fun is right at their fingertips, but instead of taking bong hits in a stolen car or getting pregnant in a neighbor's toolshed, they've come to a bookstore to hear a middle-aged man read out loud. And for that they deserve a token of my gratitude. The beauty of pain relievers is that they're light and easy to pack. On top of that, they're actually useful. "Here you are," I'll say to a sixteen-year-old. "Put this in your purse or glove compartment and think of me the next time you get a hangover."

In '08, my gifts were pretty paltry. I'd bought eight dozen safety pins in Greece, and while they *were* foreign, they didn't look much different from what you could get in the States. Ditto the German

Band-Aids. So when Bob mentioned Costco I felt that all my problems had been solved.

As with every big-box store in Winston-Salem, it took fifteen minutes to drive there and another fifteen minutes to cross the parking lot. If the building seemed large from the outside, inside it was twice as big, the kind of space that has its own weather. The carts too were slightly oversize, and made me appear even smaller than I actually am. Pushing one toward the hardware section, my brother-in-law and I looked like a pair of twelve-year-olds, the sort with that disease that speeds up the aging process and leaves them wizened and tragic.

This store didn't have the lightbulbs Bob wanted, so we trudged on to the drug section, which proved equally disappointing. Pain relievers were in ten-gallon jars rather than packets, so I looked around for another gift that a teenager might appreciate. I wanted something light and individually wrapped, and settled, finally, upon a mess of condoms, which came in a box the size of a cinder block. It was a lot of protection but not a lot of weight, and I liked that. "All right," I said to Bob. "I think these should do the trick."

Putting them in the cart, I thought nothing of it, but a moment later, walking down the aisle with my fifty-nine-year-old brother-in-law, I started feeling patently, almost titanically gay. Maybe I was imagining things, but it seemed as if people were staring at us—people in families, mostly, led by thrifty and disapproving parents who looked at what we were buying and narrowed their eyes in judgment. *You homosexuals,* their faces seemed to say. *Is that all you ever think about?*

My brother-in-law is around my height, with thick, graying hair, a matching mustache, and squarish wire-rimmed glasses. I'd never imagined him as gay, much less as my boyfriend, but now I couldn't stop. "We've got to get something else in this cart," I told him.

Bob disappeared into the acreage reserved for produce and returned a minute later with a four-pound box of strawberries. This somehow made us look even gayer. "After anal sex, we like shortcake!" read the cartoon bubble now floating over our heads.

"Something else," I said. "We've got to get something else."

Bob, oblivious, looked up at the rafters and thought for a moment. "I guess I could use some olive oil."

"Forget it," I told him, my voice a bark. "Let's just pay up and go. Can we do that, please?"

I'd later wonder what the TSA inspectors must have thought. My tour began and every few days, upon arriving in some new city, I'd find a slip of paper in my suitcase, the kind they throw in after going through all your stuff. Five dress shirts, three pairs of pants, underwear, a Dopp kit full of Band-Aids and safety pins, two neckties, and several hundred rubbers—what sort of person does the mind cobble together from these ingredients?

As the weeks passed, my suitcase grew more and

more conventional. "I've got something for you," I'd say to a teenager. "It's nothing huge, just a little something to show I care."

The kids who went to good schools would roll their eyes. "I can get those in the health room," they'd tell me.

And, in the voice of a person whose upbringing was so fundamentally different that he might as well have been raised by camel herders, I would say, "Really? For free?"

Unlike a lot of authors I know, I enjoy my book tours—love them, as a matter of fact. That said, I'm in a fortunate position, and have been able to eliminate the parts that don't agree with me—the picture-taking, for instance. People all have cameras on their cell phones now, and, figuring, I guess, that they might as well aim them at something, they'd ask me to stand and pose a good thirty times a night. This wasn't an inconvenience so much as an embarrassment. "You can do better than me," I'd tell them. And when they insisted that they really couldn't, I'd feel even worse. Thus, at readings, there's now a notice propped atop my book-signing table. "Sorry," it announces, "but we don't allow photos." This makes it sound like it's the store's idea, a standard policy, like no eating fudge in the fine-arts section.

"If it's their rule, I guess I'll have to go along with it," I tell people, sighing as if I were really disappointed.

With the picture-taking out of the way, I'm completely free to enjoy myself, which I generally do—and immensely. Every night, after a reading and a short question-and-answer session, I'll sit and talk to hundreds of strangers. This fellow, for instance, whom I met in Toronto—I liked his glasses, and, after I asked where he had gotten them, we fell into the topic of corrective surgery. "I hear that you have to remain conscious during the procedure," he told me, "and that when the laser hits its target, you can actually smell your own eyeball sizzling."

I thought about this for days, just as I thought of the special-ed teacher I met in Pittsburgh. "You know," I said, "I hear those words and automatically think, *Handicapped,* or, *Learning disabled.* But aren't a lot of your students just assholes?"

"You got it," she said. Then she told me about a kid—last day of class—who wrote on the blackboard, "Mrs. J_____ is a cock master."

I was impressed because I'd never heard that term before. She was impressed because the boy had spelled it correctly.

For hours each night I would talk to people, asking pretty much whatever I wanted. The trick, of course, is to match the right person with the right question. Take this young woman I met in Boston a few years back. I'd been signing for almost six hours, and when she finally stepped up to the table, my mind went blank. "When, um...when did you last touch a monkey?" I asked.

I expected "Never" or "It's been years," but instead she took a step back, saying, "Oh, can you smell it on me?"

The young woman's name was Jennifer, and it turned out that she worked for Helping Hands, an organization that trains monkeys to toil as slaves for paralyzed people. At her invitation, I visited the facility outside Boston and spent a pleasant afternoon having my pockets picked by some of the cleverer students.

On that tour, my questions were pretty standard: "What was the last reading you attended?" "Who are you going to use this condom on?" "If you stepped out of the shower and saw a leprechaun standing at the base of your toilet, would you scream, or would you innately understand that he meant you no harm?"

Late at night I'd return to my room, scoop up the shampoos and conditioners replaced as part of the turndown service, and record everything that I had learned, not just the stories that people had told me but all the ephemera: The names of local restaurants and hair salons seen from the car window. One hotel with its Martini Tuesdays, another with its Fajita Fridays. In Baton Rouge, a woman asked me to name her donkey. "Stephanie," I said, and later that night, too tired to sleep, I lay awake and wondered if I'd spoken too quickly.

In 2004, I offered priority signing to smokers, the reason being that, because they didn't have as long to live, their time was more valuable. Four years later my special treatment was reserved for men who stood five-foot-six and under. "That's right, my little friends," I announced. "There'll be no waiting in line for you." It seemed unfair to restrict myself to men, so I included any woman with braces on her teeth.

"What about us?" asked the pregnant and the lame. And because it was my show, I told them to wait their fucking turn.

After a month in the United States, I flew to Canada to finish my tour. On my first night in Toronto, I read at a chain store called Indigo. That event ended at midnight, and the next afternoon, following a half dozen radio and print interviews, I was taken to Costco, not to buy pain relievers and condoms but to meet my readers. Or, rather, *not* meet them. My appearance had been advertised by way of flyer and was to last no longer than an hour. Shoppers passed with their enormous carts, most loaded with children who gaped through the bars at this ridiculous nobody, sitting by himself at a folding table. Making it just that much more pathetic was the sign next to me, the big one reading "No Photos, Please."

It would be my greatest pleasure not to take your picture, I imagined people thinking. *I mean, really, just who the hell do you think you are?*

It's a question well suited to a cavernous space. There your eyes can roam heavenward, past the signs for frozen food and automotive supplies, past the arrow pointing to the cash registers, and on to that boundless parking lot, which leads, eventually, to home.

Obama!!!!!

Our village in Normandy is too small to have its own paper, but there are several that serve the region and come out once a week. If it's not that hard to get written up in, say, the *Atlanta Journal-Constitution*, it's really, *really* not hard to find yourself in *L'Orne Combattante*. In fact, it's hard to stay out of it.

The farmer across the road from us, Robert "Bob" Gerbenne, was profiled in the late 1990s. "The Man Who *Truly* Whispers to Horses," read the headline. The picture was of him, seeming to gossip into the ear of his Percheron, a dappled mare as solid as a dump truck. Hugh's been in the paper as well—twice, as a matter of fact. The last story was about his landscape paintings, and the one before that appeared in October 2004. They wanted to talk to an American about the presidential election, a who-do-you-hope-will-win sort of thing. The resulting article, titled something subtle like "Local Man Distrusts and Despises Bush," was, said the Horse Whisperer, *"pas mal,"* meaning "not bad."

Weeks before the 2008 election, the *Combattante* interviewed our friend Mary Beth, who was born and raised outside Boston and moved to our area after marrying her French husband. "Being a white American, you wouldn't vote for a black man, would you?" the reporter asked.

Though crudely phrased, the question was fairly common, and not just in backwater Normandy. In the year before the election, I traveled pretty much nonstop: Italy, Greece, Germany, the Netherlands, Australia, Brazil, and all through the U.K. and Ireland. These were book tours, so I sat for a lot of radio and print interviews. In the U.S., unless you've written about politics, you don't expect political questions. Overseas, on the other hand, it's pretty much *all* you get, at least if you're an American. I could have written a history of frosting and still they'd have asked me about Guantánamo, and my country's refusal to sign the Kyoto Accords.

It's not that I don't have opinions about these things; I just don't feel they're in any way special. Sure, I follow the news. I read the papers and listen to the radio, but I'm not privy to any inside information. When it comes to politics, all I can offer is emotion. My perspective might be slightly different, but so is anyone's when they live overseas.

I remember my dad calling after the Iraq war started and asking if I felt safe on the streets of Paris. He had the idea that the Europeans, and specifically the French, had become openly hostile and were targeting Americans—even throwing bottles at them. If that was happening, I neither saw it nor read about it. In my experience, people were curious. They had plenty of questions, but I was never insulted or singled out in any way. It might have felt different were I a Bush supporter, but as it was, the president brought my neighbors and me together. It was like the Small World pavilion at Disneyland, everyone on the same page.

As the 2008 primaries began, so did the predictions. The reporters in Greece, the ones in Australia and Amsterdam and Dublin, all of them assured me that America would never elect a black president.

"Maybe," I said, "but I'll bet you that *half* of America could elect a half-black president."

"No way," said the German who'd once spent a week in Los Angeles, the Brazilian whose wife was from Tennessee, the Englishman who'd seen *Borat* four times. Everyone was an expert, and what they all knew was this: Americans are racist.

It always sounds false when white people talk about how gentle and color-blind they are. "One thing I've learned from my many Asian, Latino, and African American friends is that we're all brothers under the skin." Statements like this make me queasy, but they're really no worse than the often heard "How could I be racist when my first boyfriend was black?"

My first boyfriend was black as well, but that doesn't prove I'm color-blind, just that I like big butts.

If I'm walking down an American street and anyone darker than a peanut shell approaches, I'll say, "Hello." This because, if I *don't* say it, he or she might think that I'm anxious. Which, of course, I must be, otherwise I'd walk by in silence, just as I do with my fellow Caucasians.

Does this make me rac*ist,* or simply race *conscious?* Either way, I'm more afraid of conservatives than I am of black people. I think a lot of Americans are. Thus, when questioned by foreign journalists, I'd predict with confidence that Obama would win.

This would get me a shake of the head and a look that translated in five languages to "Poor dreamer."

As in every election since 1998, I voted absentee and spent the month of October traveling across the United States on a lecture tour. It was all presidential campaign all the time, and what I liked was the directness of it. In France there's a far-right political party called the National Front. Blame the immigrants, stop building mosques, down with the EU: their policies are fairly predictable. The National Front's then leader, Jean-Marie Le Pen, defined the Nazi occupation of his country as "not particularly inhumane" and had twenty-five convictions against him, an assortment ranging from grievous bodily harm to anti-Semitism to condoning war crimes. He's an older guy, pale, his eyes made small by thick-lensed glasses.

When political campaigns are held in France, you see posters on the street, but they're rarely attached to a home or business, the way they are in the States.

Drive through any American city in the month before an election, and every other house will have a sign in front of it. So-and-so for president, for county commissioner, for town slut, etc. I also appreciate that Americans wear campaign buttons—identifiers saying either "You and I are alike," "I am a huge asshole," or, in the case of a third-party nominee, "I don't mind wasting my vote." It makes everyone so wonderfully easy to pigeonhole. I only wish that the buttons could be larger, the size of plates, at least. That way you could read them from a greater distance and have more time to activate your scowl. Still, it beats what you get in France, which is nothing. No pins, no bumper stickers. You can't ask people who they voted for either. It's considered rude.

I thought about this in 2002, when Jean-Marie Le Pen won a primary in our village. After the votes were tallied, I took a walk, looking into the windows of people I thought I knew and thinking, *You? Really?* Those same neighbors unwilling to discuss their own election were, of course, more than happy to talk about mine. After the 2008 conventions it was *all* we talked about. "So who are you voting for, Obama or McCain?" they wanted to know.

I said to Hugh, "They have to *ask?*" I mean, really, you'd hope it would be evident.

After my month in the United States, I flew back to France, arriving on the morning of November 4, just as Americans were going to the polls. At Charles de Gaulle Airport, I caught a cab. The driver was listening to talk radio, and during my long ride into Paris, the callers explained why my candidate could never win. "Americans are racist," they said. "Americans are afraid of anything different." You'd think that Obama was the French candidate for president of the United States, that's how possessive and prematurely disappointed everyone was. The cab driver got into it as well. "Who do you think will win?" he asked, and when I said Obama, he told me flat out that it was not going to happen.

So then, of course, it *did* happen. And everyone was like, "Obama!" Even people I didn't personally know, cashiers at the supermarket and such who identified me by my accent. "Obama!" they cried, and, "You did good." I'd like to say that their tone was congratulatory, but there was something else in there as well. Not "How wonderful that you have a thoughtful new president" but "How wonderful that you elected the president we thought you should elect."

I was in London during the inauguration and watched the ceremony on the BBC, which reminded me every three seconds that Barack Obama was black and would become America's first black president. At first I thought that this was for blind people, a little reminder in case they forgot. Then it became laughable: *Barack Obama, who is black, is arriving now with his black wife and two black children, a group that will form America's first black First Family, which is to say, the first group of blacks elected to the White House, which is white and not black like them.*

It got on my nerves, but then I thought, *If America elected its first gay president, I might want to hear it a few thousand times.* It might *take* a few thousand mentions just to sink in. For me, Obama's race had nothing to do with my voting for him. I liked that he could deliver a speech, this as opposed to our previous two Democratic candidates, both of whom spoke as if they were reading the words phonetically in Korean and didn't know where to put the emphasis.

In the last month of the presidential campaign, I tuned in to conservative talk radio and listened as callers considered the unthinkable. One after another, they all threatened the same thing: "If McCain doesn't win, I'm leaving the country."

"Oh, *right,*" I'd say. "You're going to leave and go where? Right-wing Europe?" In the Netherlands now, I imagine it's legal to marry your own children. Get them pregnant, and you can abort your unborn grandbabies in a free clinic that used to be a church. The doctor might be a woman who became a man and then became a woman again, all on taxpayers' dollars, but as long as she saves the stem cells, she'll have the nation's blessing.

That's just me, though, being insensitive. Certain people might brand me "mean-spirited," though I think that's the pot calling the kettle black. States vote to take away my marriage rights, and even though I don't want to get married, it tends to hurt my feelings. I guess what bugs me is that it was put to a vote in the first place. If you don't want to marry a homosexual, then don't. But what gives you the right to weigh in on your neighbor's options? It's like voting on whether or not redheads should be allowed to celebrate Christmas.

Of course, Obama too was against gay marriage. Except for a couple of decided long shots, all the candidates that year were. Being for it was the kiss of death, which, again, can't help but tick me off. I mean, honestly, *that's* the deciding issue? Many of those who have fought and voted against it are Democrats, and that depresses me as well. But you pick and you choose, don't you? Some things you can sit on, and others you can't. While waiting for my party to come around, I listened to my French neighbors, all of them joyous and patting me on the back. "Obama!" they cried. "Obama! Obama!" I offered in return an increasingly forced smile, thinking, *Oh, get your own black president.*

Standing By

It was one of those headaches that befall every airline passenger. A flight is delayed because of thunderstorms or backed-up traffic — or maybe it's canceled altogether. Maybe you board two hours late, or maybe you board on time and spend the next two hours sitting on the runway. When it happens to you it's a national tragedy — *Why aren't the papers reporting this?* you wonder.

Only when it happens to someone else do you realize what a dull story it really is. "They told us we'd leave at three instead of two thirty, so I went to get a frosted-pecan wrap, and when I came back they changed the time to four on account of the plane we'd be riding on hadn't left Pittsburgh yet. Then I was like, 'Why didn't you tell us that an hour ago?' and they were like, 'Ma'am, just stand away from the counter, please.'"

Because I'm in the air so often, I hear this sort of thing a lot. In line for a coffee. In line for a newspaper or a gunpowder test on the handle of my public radio tote bag: everywhere I go someone in an eight-dollar T-shirt is whipping out a cell phone and delivering the fine print of his or her delay. One can't help but listen in, but then my focus shifts and I find myself staring. I should be used to the way Americans dress when traveling, yet it still manages to amaze me. It's as if the person next to you had been washing shoe polish off a pig, then suddenly threw down his sponge saying, "Fuck this. I'm going to Los Angeles!"

On Halloween, when I see the ticket agents dressed as hags and mummies, I no longer think, *Nice costume,* but, *Now we have to tag our own luggage?*

I mean that I mistake *them* for *us.*

The scariness, of course, cuts both ways. I was on a plane in the spring of 2003 when the flight attendant asked us to pray for our troops in Iraq. It was a prickly time, but brand-new war or no brand-new war, you don't ever want to hear the word "pray" from a flight attendant.

You don't want to hear the phrase "I'll be right back" either. That's code for "Go fuck yourself," according to a woman who used to fly for Northwest and taught me several terms specific to her profession.

"You know how a plastic bottle of water will get all crinkly during a flight?" she asked. "Well, it happens to people too, to our insides. That's why we get all gassy."

"All right," I said.

"So what me and the other gals would sometimes

do is fart while we walked up and down the aisle. No one could hear it on account of the engine noise, but anyway that's what we called 'crop dusting.'"

When I asked another flight attendant, this one male, how he dealt with a plane full of belligerent passengers, he said, "Oh, we have our ways. The next time you're flying and are about to land, listen closely as we make our final pass through the cabin."

In the summer of 2009, I was trying to get from North Dakota to Oregon. There were thunderstorms in Colorado, so we were two hours late leaving Fargo. This caused me to miss my connecting flight, and upon my arrival in Denver I was directed to the customer service line. It was a long one—thirty, maybe thirty-five people, all of them cranky and exhausted. In front of me stood a woman in her midseventies, accompanying two beautifully dressed children, a boy and a girl. "The airlines complain that nobody's traveling, and then you arrive to find your flight's been oversold!" the woman griped. "I'm trying to get me and my grandkids to San Francisco, and now they're telling us there's nothing until tomorrow afternoon."

At this, her cell phone rang. The woman raised it to her ear, and a great many silver bracelets clattered down her arm. "Frank? Is that you? What did you find out?"

The person on the other end fed her information, and as she struggled to open her pocketbook, I held out my pad and pen. "A nice young man just gave me something to write with, so go ahead," the woman said. "I'm ready." Then she said, "*What?* Well, *I* could have told you that." She handed me back my pad and pen and, rolling her eyes, whispered, "Thanks anyway." After hanging up she turned to the kids. "Your old grandmother is so sorry for putting you through this. But she's going to make it up to you, she swears."

They were like children from a catalog. The little girl's skirt was a red-and-white check, and matched the ribbon that banded her straw hat. Her brother was wearing a shirt and tie. It was a clip-on, but still it made him and his sister the best-dressed people in line, much better than the family ten or so places ahead of them. That group consisted of a couple in their midfifties and three teenagers, two of whom were obviously brothers. The third teenager, a girl, was holding a very young baby. I suppose it could have been a loaner, but the way she engaged with it—the obvious pride and pleasure she was radiating—led me to believe that the child was hers. Its father, I guessed, was the kid standing next to her. The young man's hair was almost orange and drooped from his head in thin, lank braids. At the end of each one, just above the rubber band, was a colored bead the size of a marble. Stevie Wonder wore his hair like that in the late '70s, but he's black. And blind. Then too, Stevie Wonder didn't have acne on his neck and wear baggy denim shorts that fell midway between his knees and his ankles. Topping it off was the kid's T-shirt. I couldn't see the front of it, but printed in large letters across the back were the words "Freaky Mothafocka."

I didn't know where to start with that one. Let's see, I'm flying on a plane with my parents and my infant son, so should I wear the T-shirt that says, "Orgasm Donor," "Suck All You Want, I'll Make More," or, no, seeing as I'll have the beaded cornrows, I think I should go with "Freaky Mothafocka."

As the kid reached over and took the baby from the teenage girl, the woman in front of me winced. "Typical," she groaned.

"I beg your pardon."

She gestured toward the Freaky Mothafocka. "The only ones *having* babies are the ones who *shouldn't* be having them." Her gaze shifted to the adults. "And look at the stupid grandparents, proud as punch."

It was one of those situations I often find myself in while traveling. Something's said by a stranger I've been randomly thrown into contact with, and I want to say, "Listen. I'm with you on most of this, but before we continue, I need to know who you voted for in the last election."

If the grandmother's criticism was coming from the same place as mine, if she was just being petty and judgmental, we could go on all day, perhaps even form a friendship. If, on the other hand, it was tied to a conservative agenda, I was going to have to switch tracks and side with the Freaky Mothafocka, who was, after all, just a kid. He may have looked like a Dr. Seuss character, but that didn't mean he couldn't love his baby—a baby, I told myself, who just might grow up to be a Supreme Court justice or the president of the United States. Or, at least, I don't know, someone with a job.

Of course you can't just *ask* someone whom they voted for. Sometimes you can tell by looking, but the grandmother with the many bracelets could have gone either way. In the end, I decided to walk the center line. "What gets me is that they couldn't even spell 'motherfucker' right," I whispered. "I mean, what kind of example is that setting for our young people?"

After that, she didn't want to talk anymore, not even when the line advanced and Mothafocka and company moved to one of the counter positions. Including the baby, there were six in their party, so I knew it was going to take forever. *Where do they need to go, anyway?* I asked myself. *Wherever it is, would it have killed them to drive?*

Fly enough, and you learn to go brain-dead when you have to. It's sort of like time travel. One minute you're bending to unlace your shoes, and the next thing you know you're paying fourteen dollars for a fruit cup, wondering, *How did I get here?*

No sooner had I alienated the grandmother in Denver than I was trapped by the man behind me, who caught my eye and, without invitation, proceeded to complain. He had been passed over for a standby seat earlier that morning and was not happy about it. "The gal at the gate said she'd call my name when it came time to board, but hell, she didn't call me."

I tried to look sympathetic.

"I should have taken her name," the man continued. "I should have reported her. Hell, I should have punched her is what I should have done!"

"I hear you," I said.

Directly behind him was a bald guy with a silver mustache, one of those elaborate jobs that wander awhile before eventually morphing into sideburns. The thing was as curved and bushy as a squirrel's tail, and the man shook crumbs from it as the fellow who'd lost his standby seat turned to engage him.

"Goddamn airline. It's no wonder they're all going down the toilet."

"None of them want to work, that's the problem," the bald man with the mustache said. "All any of them care about is their next goddamn coffee break." He looked at the counter agents with disdain and then turned his eye on the Freaky Mothafocka. "That one must be heading back to the circus."

"Pathetic," the man behind me said. He himself was wearing pleated khaki shorts and a blue T-shirt. A baseball cap hung from his waistband, and his sneakers, which were white, appeared to be brand-new. Like a lot of men you see these days, he looked like a boy, suddenly, shockingly, set into an adult body. "We got a kid looks like him back in the town I come from, and every time I see him I just thank God he isn't mine."

As the two started in on rap music and baggy trousers, I zoned out and thought about my last layover in Denver. I was on the people mover, jogging toward my connection at the end of Concourse C, when the voice over the PA system asked Adolf Hitler to pick up a white courtesy phone. *Did I hear that correctly?* I remember thinking. It's hard to imagine anyone calling their son Adolf Hitler, so the person must have changed it from something less provocative, a category that includes pretty much everything. Weirder still was hearing the name in the same sentence as the word "courtesy." I imagined a man picking up the receiver, his voice made soft by surprise and the possibility of bad news. "Yes, hello, this is Adolf Hitler."

Thinking of it made me laugh, and that brought me back to the present and the fellow behind me in the khaki shorts. "Isn't it amazing how quickly one man can completely screw up a country?" he said.

"You got that right," Mr. Mustache agreed. "It's a goddamn mess is what it is."

I assumed they were talking about George Bush but gradually realized it was Barack Obama, who had, at that point, been in office for less than six months.

The man with the mustache mentioned a GM dealership in his hometown. "They were doing fine, but now the federal government's telling them they have to close. Like this is Russia or something, a Communist country!"

The man in the khaki shorts joined in, and I wished I'd paid closer attention to the auto bailout stuff. It had been on the radio and in all the papers, but because I don't drive and I always thought that car dealerships were ugly, I'd let my mind wander or moved on to the next story, which was unfortunate, since I'd have loved to have turned around and given those two what for. Then again, even if I were informed, what's the likelihood of changing anyone's opinion, especially a couple of strangers'? If my own little mind is nailed shut, why wouldn't theirs be?

"We've got to take our country back," the man with the mustache said. "That's the long and short of it, and if votes won't do the trick then maybe we need to use force."

What struck me with him, and with many of the conservatives I'd heard since the election, was his overblown, almost egocentric take on political outrage, his certainty that no one else had quite experienced it before. What, then, had I felt during the Bush-Cheney years? Was that somehow secondary? "Don't tell me I don't know how to hate," I wanted to say. Then I stopped and asked myself, *Do you really want* that *to be your message? Think you can out-hate me, asshole? I was fucking hating people before you were even born!*

We're forever blaming the airline industry for turning us into monsters: it's the fault of the ticket agents, the baggage handlers, the slowpokes at the newsstands and the fast-food restaurants. But what if this is who we truly are, and the airport's just a forum that allows us to be our real selves, not just hateful but gloriously so?

Would Adolf Hitler please meet his party at Baggage Claim Four? Repeat. Adolf Hitler can meet his party at Baggage Claim Four.

It's a depressing thought, and one that proved hard to shake. It was with me when I boarded my flight to Portland and was still on my mind several hours later, when we were told to put our tray tables away and prepare for landing. Then the flight attendants, garbage bags in hand, glided down the aisle, looking each one of us square in the face and whispering, without discrimination, "Your trash. You're trash. Your family's trash."

I Break for Traditional Marriage

When a referendum was passed making it legal for gay men and lesbians to marry each other in nearby New York State, the first thing my wife and I thought was *What now?*

We'd been Mr. and Mrs. Randolph Denny for going on thirty-nine years, and suddenly, on the whim of some high-and-mighty fat cats, it was all meaningless: our wedding, our anniversaries, even our love. "Who are we?" Brenda cried.

And I looked at her thinking, *What do you mean, "we"?*

Then I walked into the kitchen and yelled for my daughter, Bonita, who was watching TV in the basement rec room. You'd think that at thirty-seven she'd be married with a home and a family of her own, but when she was a teenager she fell in with a custodian at her high school. Next came the news that she was pregnant. The fetus got lodged in her tubes somehow, and to make a long story short they had to yank everything out, leaving her infertile, which is

what she deserved, if you ask her mother and me—
a custodian, for God's sake! Oh, she married him all
right, we saw to that, but two years later their relationship ended in divorce. Her next marriage ended
the same way, as did the one after that. So now here
she is, practically middle-aged and living with her
parents.

"Bonita," I yelled, "get up here."

She's lazy as sin, my daughter, and in the time it
took her to get off the sofa and climb the seven steps
to the kitchen, I was more than ready for her.

"Damn it, Daddy, I was just in the middle of—" and
before she could finish I shot her through the head. The
high jinks in New York made a sham of my marriage,
so it logically made the fruits of that marriage meaningless as well. That was one good thing that came of it.

The noise of the gun brought Brenda down from
the bedroom. "What in God's name have you done
to our daughter?" she asked. And I shot her in the
head as well, just like I'd been wanting to every day
for the past thirty-nine years.

This might sound inexcusable, but if homosexual-
ity is no longer a sin, then who's to say that murder
is? If it feels good, do it—that's what the state legislators seem to be saying. Who cares what all the
decent people think?

After shooting my wife and daughter, I grabbed
an ice pick and headed out to the garage. A few years
back my mother-in-law—Nancy Anne, she likes me
to call her—fell out of a tree. She'd been climbing
up after her iguana when a branch snapped off, and
the next thing she knew she was laid up in the hos-

pital with a dozen pins in her hip. Brenda insisted she come live with us, but what with the stairs, the house was too much of a hassle. So we moved the cars out onto the lawn and turned the garage into an apartment. She's got a kitchenette, a shower stall, the whole nine yards. You'd think it would make her happy, living there for free the way she does, but all I ever hear is that it's not insulated and hasn't got any windows. "You hung my doggone pictures on the re-tractable door, and every time someone opens it they fall off," she says.

I say, "Secure them with tape, why don't you?"

And she says, "I'm not spending my hard-earned money on tape." As if she ever worked a day in her life. She lives off alimony.

"Oh, Nancy Anne," I called, and I pointed the re-mote in the direction of her retractable door. She was in her nightgown but had tights on underneath it— in this heat! Her glasses were on top of the TV set, and she reached for them, saying, "Randolph? Ran-dolph, is that you?"

Boy, it felt good to reclaim that garage. After drag-ging Nancy Anne's bed into the backyard, I returned for her sofa, then her potty-chair. I got her clothes, her cushions, all of her wooden bracelets and hair-pieces, and built a raging bonfire. Then I threw her body into the flames and returned my cars to their rightful place. Or what I thought of as their rightful place. For all I knew, in the time it took to kill my mother-in-law with an ice pick and throw her onto a

bonfire, some activist judge or group of state assem-
blymen had decided that cars don't *belong* in garages
anymore, that they should live in houses and eat
chicken dinners, just like people do. Up was down
and down was up, as far as the world was concerned,
so why not make like the homosexuals and follow
my dreams?

Back in the house, I made a list. Everything I'd
always wanted to do but didn't because society
frowned on it:

1. Shoot my wife.

That I could cross off, along with:

2. Solve the Bonita problem, and
3. Stab Nancy Anne through the eye with an
   ice pick.

Next I needed to:

4. Grow a mustache like Yosemite Sam's.
5. Make a piñata but use precious documents instead of torn newspaper.
6. Eat at the Old Spaghetti Factory and walk
   out without paying.

There are other things I'd like to do, but this, I
figured, was more than enough to start with. Seeing
as the Old Spaghetti Factory wouldn't be open until
lunchtime and there was nothing I could do to rush
the mustache, I decided to start by going to the

bank and withdrawing some precious documents. The marriage license in my safe-deposit box was no longer worth the paper it was printed on, but that still left my birth certificate, my life insurance policy, and my social security card.

While driving to First Federal, I listened to the radio, an all-talk program I'm partial to where the callers were just as riled up as I was.

When I tuned in, Sherry was on the line. "If the gays can stand in a church of God and exchange vows, who's to say my husband can't divorce me and marry a five-year-old?" she said. "Or a newborn baby, heaven forbid! I'm not saying he's into that, but I guess if he was, there'd be nothing stopping him now!"

The next caller identified himself as Steverino. "I remember as a boy we had this joke," he said. "Your buddy might say, 'I love this pepperoni pizza,' and you'd say, 'Why don't you marry it, then?'

"At the time it was just a saying, but I guess now you really *could* tie the knot with a pizza, couldn't you? I mean, if the guy who cuts my mother's hair is free to wed his little gay boyfriend, why can't I marry a slab of flattened-out dough with cheese and dried sausage on it?"

The host of the show is a guy named Jimbo Barnes, and on pretty much everything we see eye-to-eye. "There's no reason I can think of why you couldn't marry a pizza," he said. "Hell, you could probably even marry a mini-pizza, one of those ones made from an English muffin, if you felt like it."

Steverino said that he didn't really like English

muffins, and Jimbo said that was just an example. "Bite-size pizza or sixteen-incher, whatever floats your boat is what the activist state legislatures are saying."

This was something I'd never thought of—marrying an object: my refrigerator, say, or maybe the riding mower I sometimes borrowed from my neighbor Pete Spaker. It's a John Deere X304—top-of-the-line, with automatic transmission, cruise control, and four-wheel steering. Maybe I could just borrow it again, and when he asked me to return it, I'd tell him we'd eloped, that the mower was my new wife and until such time as we divorced, it was living with me!

Of course, by then they'd have probably closed the loopholes. Taking away anything that might benefit traditional heterosexuals, especially white ones and especially *especially* white males. This is something Jimbo Barnes addresses quite often—"an endangered species," he calls us. No matter that we made this country what it is today. Thinking about this got me so mad that I missed my turnoff for the bank. This meant taking a side street, where I fell in behind a school bus, of all things.

I know you're not supposed to pass them, but normal classes were out for the summer, so the only students on board were ones who had failed and had to go to summer school—dummies, basically, like my daughter, Bonita, had been. The bus stopped on the corner, and just as I was pulling around it, this kid—most likely a gay one—threw himself in front of my car. Someone got my license plate number as

I was taking off, and the next thing I know, I'm in jail with one charge of second-degree manslaughter and three charges of first-degree murder! Plus the hit-and-run bit. And all because some high-and-mighty legislators in New York State thought they knew better than the rest of us! Of course, if I was gay they'd probably let me off, so I tried kissing my cell mate, an illegal immigrant named Diego Rodríguez, if you can believe it.

And I'm here to tell you that, as long as you keep your eyes shut, it's really not that bad.

Understanding
Understanding Owls

Does there come a day in every man's life when he looks around and says to himself, *I've got to weed out some of these owls?* I can't be alone in this, can I? And, of course, you don't want to hurt anyone's feelings. Therefore you keep the crocheted owl given to you by your second-youngest sister and accidentally on purpose drop the mug that reads "Owl Love You Always" and was sent by someone who clearly never knew you to begin with. I mean, mugs with words on them! Owl cocktail napkins stay, because everyone needs napkins. Ditto owl candle. Owl trivet: take to the charity shop along with the spool-size Japanese owl that blinks his eyes and softly hoots when you plug him into your computer.

Just when you think you're making progress, you remember the owl tobacco tin and the owl tea cozy. Then there are the plates, the coasters, the Christmas ornaments. This is what happens when you tell people you like something. For my sister Amy, that thing was rabbits. When she was in her late thirties, she got one as a pet, and before it had chewed through its first phone cord, she'd been given rabbit slippers, cushions, bowls, refrigerator magnets, you name it. "Really," she kept insisting, "the live one is enough." But nothing could stem the tide of crap.

Amy's invasion started with a live rabbit, while Hugh's and mine began, in the late 1990s, with decorative art. We were living in New York then, and he had his own painting business. One of his clients had bought a new apartment, and on the high, domed ceiling of her entryway she wanted a skyful of birds. Hugh began with warblers and meadowlarks. He sketched some cardinals and blue tits for color and was just wondering if it wasn't too busy when she asked if he could add some owls. It made no sense naturewise—owls and songbirds work different shifts, and even if they didn't they would still never be friends. No matter, though. This was her ceiling, and if she wanted turkey vultures—or, as was later decided, bats—that's what she would get. All Hugh needed was a reference, so he went to the Museum of Natural History and returned with *Understanding Owls*. The book came into our lives almost fifteen years ago, and I've yet to go more than a month without mentioning it. "You know," I'll say. "There's something about nocturnal birds of prey that I *just don't get*. If only there was somewhere I could turn for answers."

"I wish I could help you," Hugh will say, adding, a second or two later, "Hold on a minute...what about...*Understanding Owls*?"

We've performed this little routine more times

than I can count, but back then, when the book was still fresh-smelling and its pages had not yet yellowed, I decided that because Hugh actually *did* get a kick out of owls, I would try to find him a stuffed one. My search turned up plenty of ravens. I found pheasants and ducks, and foot-tall baby ostriches. I found a freeze-dried turkey's head attached to its own foot, but owls, no luck. That's when I learned that it's illegal to own them in the United States. Even if one dies naturally of a stroke or old age. If it chokes on a mouse or gets kicked by a horse. Should one fly against your house, break its neck, and land like magic on your front stoop, you're still not allowed to stuff it or even to store its body in your freezer. Technically, you're not even allowed to keep one of its feathers—that's how protected they are. I learned this at a now-defunct taxidermy shop in midtown Manhattan. "But if you're *really* interested," the clerk I spoke to said, "I've got a little something you might want to see." He stepped into the back room and returned with what I could only identify as a creature. "What we've done," he boasted, "is stretch a chicken over an owl *form*."

"That's really...something," I said, groping for a compliment. The truth was that even a child would have seen this for what it was. The beak made from what looked to be a bear claw, the feet with their worn-down, pedestrian talons: I mean, *please!* This was what a chicken might wear to a Halloween party if she had ten minutes to throw a costume together. "Let me think about it," I said.

*   *   *

Years later we moved to Paris, where, within my first week, I found an albino peacock. I found swans and storks and all manner of seabirds but, again, no owls, because stuffing them is forbidden in France. In the U.K., though, it's a slightly different story. You can't go out and shoot one, certainly. They're protected in life just as they are in the U.S., but afterward, in death, things loosen up a bit. Most of the owls I saw in Great Britain had been stuffed during the Victorian era. I'd see them at English flea markets and in Scottish antique shops, but, as is always the case, the moment you decide to buy one they're nowhere to be had. I needed one—or decided I did—in February 2008. Hugh and I were moving from our apartment to a house in Kensington, and, after going through our owl objects and deciding we could do without nine-tenths of them, I thought I'd get him the real thing for Valentine's Day. I should have started looking a month or two in advance, but with Christmas and packing and helping to ready our new place, it had slipped my mind. Thus I wound up on February 13 calling a London taxidermy shop and asking if they had any owls. The person who answered the phone told me he had two of them, both recent specimens, and freestanding, not behind glass as most of the old ones are. The store was open only by appointment, and after arranging to come by the following afternoon, I went to where Hugh was packing books in the next room and said, "I am giving you the best Valentine's Day gift *ever*."

This is one of those things I do and immediately hate myself for. How is the other person supposed to respond? What's the point? For the first sixteen years we were together, I'd give Hugh chocolates for Valentine's Day, and he'd give me a carton of cigarettes. Both of us got exactly what we wanted, and it couldn't have been easier. Then I quit smoking and decided that in place of cigarettes I needed, say, an eighteenth-century scientific model of the human throat. It was life-size, about four inches long, and, because it was old, handmade, and designed to be taken apart for study, it cost quite a bit of money. "When did Valentine's Day turn into *this*?" Hugh asked when I told him that he had to buy it for me.

What could I say? Like everything else, holiday gifts escalate. The presents get better and better until one year you decide you don't need anything else and start making donations to animal shelters. Even if you hate dogs and cats, they're somehow *always* the ones who benefit. "Eventually we'll celebrate by spaying a few dozen kittens," I said, "but until that day comes, *I want that throat*."

On Valentine's Day, I carried a few boxes from our apartment to the house we'd bought. It looked like the sort of place where Scrooge might have lived—a narrow brick building, miserly in terms of space, and joined to identical, equally grim houses on either side of it. From there I walked around the corner and got on the Underground. The taxidermy shop was on a quiet street in North London, and as I approached I saw a man and his two sons with their faces pressed against the barred front windows. "A polar bear!" one of the boys shouted. The other tugged on his father's coat. "And a penguin! Look at the baby penguin!"

My heart raced.

The man who owned the shop was so much taller than me that, in order to look him in the eye, I had to throw my head all the way back, like I do at the dentist's office. He had enviably thick hair, and as he opened the door to let me in I noticed an orange kitten positioned on the floor beside a dalmatian puppy. Casting a shadow upon them was a rabbit standing upright on its hind legs, and above him, on a shelf, sat two tawny owls, each mounted to a stump and standing around twenty inches high. Both were females, and in great shape, but what I'd really wanted was a barn owl. Those are the ones with spooky white faces, like satellite dishes with eyes.

"We do get those from time to time, but they're rare," the taxidermist said. Above his head hung a massive seagull with its beak open, and next to him, on a tabletop, lounged a pair of hedgehogs.

I've seen better variety, but there was no denying that the man did beautiful work. Nothing had crooked eyes or bits of exposed plaster at the corners of its mouth. If seen in a photo, you'd think that these animals were alive and had gathered peacefully to boast about their excellent health. The taxidermist and I discussed the owls, and when my eyes cut to a glass-doored cabinet with several weather-beaten skulls inside it, he asked if I was a doctor.

"Me?" For some reason I looked at my hands. "Oh, goodness no."

"Then your interest in those skulls is nonprofessional?"

"Exactly."

The taxidermist's eyes brightened, and he led me to a human skeleton half hidden in the back of the room. "Who do you think this was?" he asked.

Being a layman, all I had to go by was the height—between four and a half and five feet tall. "Is it an adolescent?"

The taxidermist invited me to guess again, but before I could he blurted, "It's a Pygmy!" He then told me that in the nineteenth century the English went to what is now the Congo and hunted these people, tracked them down and shot them for sport.

Funny how quickly this changed the mood. "But he *could* have died of a heart attack, right?" I said. "I mean, how are we to know for certain that he was murdered?"

"Oh, we know, all right," the taxidermist told me. It would have been disturbing to see the skeleton of a slain Pygmy in a museum, but finding him in a shop, for sale, raised certain questions, uncomfortable ones, like *How much is he?*

"If you like the odd bits and pieces, I think I've got something else you might enjoy." The taxidermist retreated to the area behind his desk and pulled a plastic bag off an overhead shelf. It was, I noticed, from Waitrose, a grocery store described to me upon my move to England as "a cut above." From the bag he removed what looked like a platter with an oblong glass dome over it. Inside was a man's forearm, complete with little hairs and a smudged tattoo. The taxidermist said, completely unnecessarily, "Now there's a story behind this." For what human limb in a Waitrose bag is *not* without some sort of story?

He placed the platter on the table, and as the lid was lifted and set to the side, I was told that, a hundred years ago, the taxidermist's grandfather witnessed a bar fight between two sailors. One was armed with a saber, and the other, apparently, was disarmed with one. After it happened, the crowd went wild. The amputee fell on his back, and as he lay there in shock, bleeding to death, the taxidermist's grandfather looked down at the floor, at the blood-soaked fingers that may have still been twitching, and likely thought, *Well, it's not like it's doing him any good.*

The story sounds a bit far-fetched, but there was no denying that the arm was real. The cut had been made two inches south of the elbow, and the exposed end, with its cleanly severed radius and ulna, reminded me of osso buco. "It was my grandfather who mummified it," the taxidermist said. "You can see it's not the best job in the world, but it's really rather good for a first attempt."

I leaned closer.

"Touch it," he whispered.

As if I were under a spell, I did, shuddering a little at the feel of the hairs. Equally creepy was the arm's color, which was not Caucasian flesh tone but not brown either, the way most desiccated body parts are. This was the same slightly toasted shade as a spray-on tan.

"I think I'll just take one of those owls," I said. "The one on the left, if that's okay."

The taxidermist nodded. Then he reached to an even higher shelf and brought down another plastic grocery bag, this one from Tesco, which is decidedly less upscale. "Now, a smell is going to hit you when I open this up, but don't worry," he said. "It's just the smoke they used to preserve the head."

That's a phrase you don't hear too often, so it took a moment for it to sink in. When he opened the bag, I saw that he might more accurately have said "the head of this teenage girl," for she'd been no older than fourteen at the time of her death. This sounds super grisly but is, I propose, just medium grisly. The head was four hundred years old and came from somewhere in South America—Peru, I think he said. The skin was dry and thin, like leather on an old worn-out purse. Parts of it were eaten away, exposing the skull beneath it, but what really struck me was her hair, which was sleek and black, divvied into delicate, slender braids.

I didn't ask the price but said a little more emphatically, "I really think the owl will do it for me today. It's a Valentine's Day present—perfect for our new place. A house, actually—no basement, and three stories tall." I wasn't trying to be boastful. I just wanted him to know that I was loved, and that I lived aboveground.

*   *   *

A few minutes later, the owl secured in a good-size cardboard box, I headed back to the Underground. Ordinarily I'd be elated—I'd been determined to find Hugh the perfect present, and, by golly, I had done it—but instead I felt unhinged, not by the things I had seen so much as by the taxidermist. It's common to be misread by people who don't know you. "Like to try Belligerent, the new fragrance for men?" I'll be asked in a department store. And I always think, *Really? Do I seem like the kind of guy who would wear cologne?* Hotel operators so often address me as "Mrs. Sedaris" that I no longer bother to correct them. I've been mistaken for a parent, a pickpocket, and even, God forbid, an SUV owner, and I've always been able to brush it off. What's rare is *not* to be misread. The taxidermist knew me for less time than it took to wipe my feet on his mat, and, with no effort whatsoever, he looked into my soul and recognized me for the person I really am: the type who'd actually love a Pygmy and could easily get over the fact that he'd been murdered for sport, thinking breezily, *Well, it was a long time ago.* Worse still I would flaunt it, hoping in the way a Porsche owner does that this would become a part of my identity. "They say he has a Pygmy," I could imagine my new neighbors whispering as I walked down the street. "Hangs him plain as day in the corner of his living room, next to the musket he was shot with."

I'd love to be talked about in this way, but how did the taxidermist know? Plenty of people must go into his store, ask for a kitten or a seagull or whatever, and walk out five minutes later knowing nothing about the human parts. Why show *me* the head in the grocery bag? As for the arm, how had he known I'd been dying to touch it? I hadn't said anything one way or the other, so what was the give-away?

At the station I went through the turnstile and stood on the platform until a train arrived. The owl wasn't heavy—in fact it was surprisingly light—but the box was cumbersome, so I was happy to find a seat. At our first stop, a teenage girl in a school uniform got on and took the spot across from me. Deal with a kid her age today and the thought of her head winding up behind some shop counter in a plastic bag might not be all that troubling. I mean, the mouths on some of them! That said, it shouldn't be just *any* kid that age. The one the taxidermist showed me, for instance—what was *her* story? Fourteen-year-olds existed four hundred years ago, but teenagers, with their angst and rebelliousness, their rage and Ritalin and very own version of *Vogue* magazine, are a fairly recent construct. In the seventeenth-century jungles of Peru, a girl that age would have babies already. Half her life would prob-ably be over, and that's if she was lucky. To have your chopped-off head preserved and then wind up in a Tesco bag some six thousand miles away—that was the indignity. Tesco! At least the arm was in a Waitrose bag.

It bothered me that the bag bothered me more than the head did, but what are you going to do? A person doesn't consciously choose what he focuses on. Those things choose you, and, once they do, nothing, it seems, can shake them. Find someone with a similar eye, and Christmas shopping is a breeze. I can always spot something for my sisters Gretchen and Amy. The three of us can walk into a crowded party and all zoom in on the person who's missing a finger, or who has one regular-size ear and one significantly smaller one, while my sister Lisa will pick up something else entirely.

Hugh and I don't notice the same things either. That's how he can be with me. Everything the taxidermist saw is invisible to him: my superficiality, my juvenile fascination with the abnormal, my willingness to accept and sometimes even celebrate evil—point this out, and he'll say, "David? *My* David? Oh no. He's not like that at all."

A person who's that out of it deserves both an owl *and* chocolate, so I got off the train at Piccadilly Circus and picked him up a box. Then I caught a bus and hurried toward home, thinking about love, and death, and about that throat, so elegant in its detail, which was, no doubt, awaiting me.

#2 to Go

"I have to go to China," I told people, this in the way I might say, "I need to insulate my crawl space," or, "I've got to get these moles looked at." That's the way it felt, though. Like a chore. What initially put me off was the food. I'll eat it if the alternative means starving, but I've never looked forward to it, not even when it seemed exotic to me. I was in my early twenties when a Chinese restaurant opened in Raleigh. It was in a new building, designed to look vaguely templish, and my mother couldn't get enough of it. "What do you say we go Oriental!"

I think she liked that the food was beyond her range. Anyone could imitate the twice-baked potatoes at the Peddler, or turn out a veal Parmesan like the Villa Capri's, but there was no way a non-Chinese person could make moo shu pork, regardless of his or her training. "And the egg rolls," she'd say. "Can you imagine!"

The restaurant didn't have a liquor license, but they allowed you to brown-bag. Thus we'd arrive with our jug of hearty burgundy. I always got my mother to order for me, but when the kung pao chicken was brought to the table I never perked up the way I did at the steak house or the Villa Capri. And it wasn't just Raleigh's Chinese food. I was equally disinterested in Chicago and, later, New York, cities with actual Chinatowns.

Everyone swore that the food in Beijing and Chengdu would be different from what I'd had in the United States. "It's more real," they said, meaning, it turned out, that I could dislike it more authentically.

I think it hurt that before landing in China, Hugh and I spent a week in Tokyo, where the food was, as always, sublime, everything so delicate and carefully presented. With meals I drank tea, which leads me to another great thing about Japan—its bathrooms. When I was younger they wouldn't have mattered so much. Then I hit fifty and found that I had to pee all the time. In Tokyo every subway station has a free public men's room. The floors and counters are aggressively clean, and beside each urinal is a hook for hanging your umbrella.

This was what I had grown accustomed to when we flew from Narita to Beijing Capital International, where the first thing you notice is what sounds like a milk steamer, the sort a café uses when making lattes and cappuccinos. *That's odd,* you think. *There's a coffee bar on the elevator to the parking deck?* What you're hearing, that incessant guttural hiss, is the sound of one person, and then another, dredging up phlegm, seemingly from the depths of his or her soul. At first you look over, wondering, *Where are you going to put that?* A better question, you soon realize, is *Where* aren't *you going to put it?*

I saw wads of phlegm glistening like freshly shucked oysters on staircases and escalators. I saw them frozen into slicks on the sidewalk and oozing down the sides of walls. It often seemed that if people weren't spitting they were coughing without covering their mouths, or shooting wads of snot out of their noses. This was done by plugging one nostril and using the other as a blowhole. "We Chinese think it's best just to get it out," a woman told me over dinner one night. She said that, in her opinion, it's disgusting that a Westerner would use a handkerchief and then put it back into his pocket.

"Well, it's not for sentimental reasons," I told her. "We don't hold on to our snot forever. The handkerchief's mainly a sanitary consideration."

Another thing you notice in China are the turds. *Oh please,* you're probably thinking. *Must you?*

To this I answer, "Yes, I must," for if they didn't affect the food itself, they affected the way I thought about it. Once, in Tokyo, I saw a dog pee on the sidewalk. Then its owner reached into a bag, pulled out a bottle of water, and rinsed the urine off the pavement. As for dog feces, I never saw any trace of them. In Beijing you see an overwhelming amount of shit. Some of it can be blamed on pets, but a lot of it comes from people. Chinese babies do without diapers, wearing instead these strange little pants with a slit in the rear. When a child has to go, its parents direct it toward the curb or, if they're indoors, to a spot they think of as "curby." "Last month I saw a kid shit in the produce aisle of our Chengdu Walmart," a young woman named Bridget told me.

This was the seventh day of my visit, and so desensitized was I that my first response was "You have a Walmart?"

There are the wild outdoor turds of China, and then there are the ones you see in the public bathrooms, most of which feature those squat-style toilets—holes, basically, level with the floor. And these bathrooms, my God. The sorriest American gas station cannot begin to match one of these things. In the men's room of a Beijing subway stop, I watched a man walk past the urinal, lift his three-year-old son into the air, and instruct him to pee into the sink—the one we were supposed to wash our hands in.

My trip reminded me that we are all just animals, that stuff comes out of every hole we have, no matter where we live or how much money we've got. On some level we all know this and manage, quite pleasantly, to shove it toward the back of our minds. In China it's brought to the front and nailed there. The supermarket cashier holds out your change and you take it thinking, *This woman squats and spits on the floor while shitting and blowing snot out of her nose.* You think it of the cab driver, of the ticket taker, and, finally, of the people who are cooking and serving your dinner. Which brings me back to food.

If someone added a pinch of human feces to my scrambled eggs, I might not be able to detect it, but I would most likely realize that these particular eggs tasted different from the ones I had yesterday. That's with something familiar, though. And there wasn't a lot of familiar in China. No pork lo mein or kung pao chicken, and definitely no egg rolls. On our first night in Chengdu, we joined a group of four for dinner—one Chinese woman and three Westerners. The restaurant was not fancy, but it was obviously popular. Built into our table was a simmering cauldron of broth, into which we were to add side dishes and cook them until they were done. "I've taken the liberty of ordering us some tofu, some mushrooms, and some duck tongues," said the Western woman sitting across from me. "Do you trust me to keep ordering, or is there anything in particular you might like?"

I looked at her, thinking, *You whore!* Catherine was English and had lived in China for close to twenty years. I figured the duck tongues were a sort of test, so I made it a point to look unfazed. Excited even.

When I was eventually forced to eat one, I found that it actually wasn't so bad. The only disconcerting part was the shape, particularly the base, from which dangled tentacle-like roots. This reminded you that the tongues had not been cut off but, rather, yanked out, possibly with pliers. Of course, the duck was probably dead by then, wasn't it? It's not like they'd jerk out the tongue and then let it go, traumatized and quackless but otherwise whole.

It was while eating my second duck tongue that the man at the next table hacked up a loud wad of phlegm and spat it onto the floor.

"I think I'm done," I said.

*   *   *

The following morning, and with a different group, Hugh and I took a drive to the mountain where tea originally came from. It was late January, and the two-hour trip took us by countless factories. Mustard-colored smoke drifted into the sky, and the rivers we passed ran thick with waste and rubbish. Eventually we hit snow, which improved things visually but made it harder to move about. By the time we headed back down the mountain, it was almost three. Most restaurants had quit serving lunch, so we stopped at what's called a Farming Family Happiness. This is a farmhouse where, if they're in the mood, the people who live there will cook and serve you a meal.

One of the members of our party was a native of Chengdu, and of the five Americans, everyone but Hugh and I spoke Mandarin. Thus we hung back as they negotiated with the farm wife, who was square-faced and pretty and wore her hair cut into bangs. We ate in what was normally the mah-jongg parlor, a large room overlooking the family's tea field. Against one wall were two televisions, each tuned to a different channel and loudly playing to no one. On the other wall was a sanitation grade—C—and the service grade, which was a smiley face with the smile turned upside down.

As far as I know there wasn't a menu. Rather, the family worked at their convenience, with whatever was handy or in season. There was a rooster parading around the backyard, and then there just wasn't. After the cook had slit its throat, he used it as the base for five separate dishes, one of which was a dreary soup with two feet, like inverted salad tongs, sticking out of it. Nothing else was nearly as recognizable.

I'm used to standard butchering: here's the leg, the breast, etc. At the Farming Family Happiness, rather than being carved, the rooster was senselessly hacked, as if by a blind person, a really angry one with a thing against birds. Portions were reduced to shards, mostly bone, with maybe a scrap of meat attached. These were then combined with cabbage and some kind of hot sauce.

Another dish was made entirely of organs, which again had been hacked beyond recognition. The heart was there, the lungs, probably the comb and intestines as well. I don't know why this so disgusted me. If I was a vegetarian, okay, but if you're a meat eater, why draw these arbitrary lines? "I'll eat the thing that filters out toxins but not the thing that sits on top of the head, doing nothing." And why agree to eat *this* animal and not that one?

I remember reading a few years ago about a restaurant in the Guangdong Province that was picketed and shut down because it served cat. The place was called the Fangji Cat Meatball Restaurant, which isn't exactly hiding anything. Go to Fangji and you pretty much know what you're getting. My objection to cat meatballs is not that I have owned several cats and loved them, but that I try not to eat things that eat meat. Like most Westerners I tend toward herbivores and things that like grain: cows, chickens, sheep, etc. Pigs eat meat—a pig would happily eat a human—but most of the pork we're privy to was raised on corn or horrible chemicals rather than on other pigs and dead people.

There are distinctions among the grazing animal eaters as well. People who like lamb and beef, at least in North America, tend to draw the line at horse, which in my opinion is delicious. The best I've had was served at a restaurant in Antwerp, a former stable called, cleverly enough, the Stable. Hugh was right there with me, and though he ate the same thing I did, he practically wept when someone in China mentioned eating sea horses. "Oh, those poor things," he said. "How could you?"

I went, "Huh?"

It's like eating poultry but taking a moral stand against Peeps, those sugarcoated chicks they sell at Easter. "A sea horse is not related to an actual horse," I said. "They're fish, and you eat fish all the time. Are you objecting to this one because of its shape?"

He said he couldn't eat sea horses because they were friendly and never did anyone any harm. This as opposed to those devious, bloodthirsty lambs whose legs we so regularly roast with rosemary and new potatoes.

The dishes we had at the Farming Family Happiness were meant to be shared, and as the pretty woman with the broad face brought them to the table, the man across from me beamed and reached for his chopsticks. "You know," he said, "this country might have its faults, but it is virtually impossible to get a bad meal here."

I didn't say anything.

Another of the dishes that day consisted of rooster blood. I'd thought it would be liquid, like V8 juice, but when cooked it coagulated into little pads that had the consistency of tofu. "Not bad," said the girl who was seated beside me, and I watched as she slid one into her mouth. Jill was American, a peace corps volunteer who'd come to Chengdu to teach English. "In Thailand last year, I ate dog face," she told me.

"Just the face?"

"Well, head and face." She was in a small village, part of a team returning abducted girls to their parents. To show their gratitude, the locals prepared a feast. Dog was considered good eating. The head was supposedly the best part and, rather than offend her hosts, Jill ate it.

This, for many, is flat-out evil, but the rest of the world isn't like America, where it's become virtually impossible to throw a dinner party. One person doesn't eat meat, while another is lactose intolerant or can't digest wheat. You have vegetarians who eat fish and others who won't touch it. Then there are vegans, macrobiotics, and a new group, flexitarians, who eat meat if not too many people are watching. Take that into consideration, and it's actually rather refreshing that a twenty-two-year-old from the suburbs of Detroit will pick up her chopsticks and at least try the char-pei.

I'd like to be more like Jill, but in China, something kept holding me back. In clean, sophisticated Japan, the rooster blood, arranged upon a handmade plate between the perfect tempura snow pea and a radish carved to look like a first-trimester fetus, would have seemed like a fine idea. "We ought to try making this at home," I'd have said to Hugh. Here, though, I thought of the sanitation grade and of the rooster, pecking maggots out of human feces before being killed. Most of the restaurants in China smelled dirty to me, though what I was picking up on was likely some unfamiliar ingredient, and I was allowing the things I'd seen earlier in the day—the spitting and snot-blowing, etc.—to fill in the blanks.

Then again, maybe not.

While on our trip we ate at normal, everyday places and sometimes bought food on the street. Our only expensive meal was in Beijing, where we went alone to a fancy restaurant recommended by an acquaintance. The place was located in an old warehouse and had been lavishly decorated. There was a wine expert and someone whose job it was to drop by every three minutes and refill your water glass. We had the Peking duck, which was expertly carved rather than hacked and was served with little pancakes. Toward the end of the meal I stepped into the men's room to pee, and there, disintegrating in the Western-style toilet, was an unflushed turd, a little reminder saying, "See, you're still in China!"

Back at the table I asked for the bill. Then I remembered where I was and amended it to "the check." In France, you can die waiting to pay for your meal, which is something I've never understood. *How can they not want me out of here?* I'll think. Ten minutes might pass. Then twenty, me watching

as the waiter does everything but accept my goddamn money.

I'll say that for China, though, offer to pay, and
before you can stab a rooster with a rusty screwdriver someone has taken you up on it. I think they
want to catch you before you get sick, but whatever
the reason, within minutes you're back on the street,
searching the blighted horizon and wondering where
your next meal might be coming from.

Health-Care Freedoms and Why I Want My Country Back

Dear Fellow Patriot/Patriotess,

Like many of you, I'd originally planned to carry a sign. The one I'd worked on pictured a witch doctor with the face of—it kills me to say it—*our president,* with a bone through his nose and that African-type paint on his cheeks. Under that I had written, "Indonesian Muslim Welfare Thug Hands Off My Healthcare You Kenyan Socialist Baby Grandma Killer." I thought it looked pretty good, but then I ran it by my son, Todd. He's the artistic one in the family. "Well, Mom," he said to me, "it's a little... busy."

We got to talking about my concerns, and because I have so many of them, he suggested I go the flyer route. The last I heard, our God-given right to mimeograph has not been taken away—Chairman Obama's left us that, at least!—and Todd assures me that this will work just as well as a picket sign. "The key, Mom, is to hand these to as many people as possible."

He then gave me the T-shirt I'm wearing, which I unfolded and held before me to read: "Big...*Dyke?*" I said.

And Todd said, "Exactly!" A dyke, he explained, is someone who holds back the flood of encroaching socialism. And that pretty much sums me up in a nutshell! "Let's add the word 'proud' to that," I said. So out came the press-on letters, and voilà!

He's made such a turnaround, that boy of mine. Back at college he was as liberal as they come— all "Down with Bush" and "Satan/Cheney '08!" But that's what our universities do now—they brainwash.

I said, "Get out into the *real* world, then you'll see!" I said, "Pay some taxes for once in your life and you'll be mad as hell too!"

And that's exactly what happened. After graduating with a useless degree in Dance History, Todd got a job at our local community college, working in the admissions office, and when he saw the bite Uncle Sam was taking out of his paycheck, he came right around, I'll tell you what. So did his roommate, Miles. The two of them met in college and have been as thick as thieves ever since. I actually sometimes call him "Shadow," not because he's black, which he is, but because he and my son are so close. It's actually him who xeroxed these flyers for me.

Both Miles and Todd are familiar with protest marches, mostly from their misguided college days, but as my son said, "Walking is walking, Mom, and whether you're *for* torture or against it, you're going to need to drink lots of water. That's rule number one: Stay Hydrated! You'll also need some good, comfortable shoes and a hat that'll keep the sun off your face."

I got a sombrero and hung tea bags off the brim, but Todd said it sent a mixed message, like I supported illegal immigration—which I don't! He said it was better to wear this cone-shaped thing, a wimple, he called it, though it looked to me more like a dunce cap. He said, "Mom, please. A little sophistication!"

I said, "How will it keep the sun off my face?" So he added a visor to the front of it. As for the writing that runs top to bottom, it might look like ASSHOLE, but it's actually A.S.S.H.O.L.E., which stands for:

Another
Savvy
Senior
Hopes
Obama
Loses
Everything

That might sound harsh, but it's how I feel. His teeth, his family, the keys to his car—I want that man to be left with nothing, just like he's trying to leave *us* with nothing. My only worry was that it was vague, and people would think that *I* was the asshole.

"Not at all," my son told me. "It's a very common acronym, like CPAC, and everyone will know what it means." So now here I am in my Big Proud Dyke

T-shirt. I've got my cone-shaped hat on, and I'm here to say that I'm mad as hell and I want my country back. I want a Christian president who was born in America, not Africa, and I don't want a death panel telling me when I can and cannot live. Then there's the tax business, which really makes my blood boil. The way it is now, if I win the lottery I'll have to give the government a much higher percentage than I would have if I'd won it when Bush was in office.

"What else gets your goat?" Todd asked when he was typing up my flyer. And I told him I was sick of the president talking down to me. "Like I'm some kind of a . . . some kind of a . . ."

"Uninformed idiot?" he said.

And I told him that was it exactly. "I'm tired of being talked to like I'm an uninformed idiot. I think a lot of Americans are, but we'll see who's the idiot when I join that historic march on Washington!"

Todd agreed 100 percent, and then he took me to the Greyhound station, where I got on the bus for Seattle.

Now Hiring Friendly People

To those who don't travel very often, the Courtyard Marriott might seem like a decent enough hotel. It's clean, sure, and the staff is polite. I wouldn't give you two cents for its pillows, though, and the tubs are far too shallow for my taste. In the deserted lobby of one I stayed at in New Hampshire, there was a coffee bar—not a Starbucks but a place that "proudly served" Starbucks, and sold it alongside breakfast cereals and prepackaged sandwiches. I noticed it on my way back from lunch, and just as I decided to get a cup of coffee, someone came from around the corner and moved in ahead of me.

I'd later learn that her name was Mrs. Dunston, a towering, dough-colored pyramid of a woman wearing oversize glasses and a short-sleeved linen blazer. Behind her came a man I guessed to be her husband, and after looking up at the menu board, she turned to him. "A latte," she said. "Now is that the thing that Barbara likes to get, the one with whipped cream, or is that called something else?"

Oh fuck, I thought.

"I can do a latte with whipped cream on top," the young woman behind the counter said. She was fair and wore her shoulder-length hair pushed behind her ears. Tiny moles were scattered like buckshot across her face, which was bare but for a bit of eyeliner. "I can do one with flavors too."

"Really?" Mrs. Dunston said. "What sorts of flavors?"

In the end she settled on caramel. Then her husband squinted up at the board, deciding after a good long while that he'd try one of those mocha something or others. And could he get that iced?

As I groaned into my palm, he wandered off. His wife, meanwhile, leaned her bulk against the counter and began her genial interrogation. "Are you from this area?" she asked. "No? From *Vermont?* Well, that's interesting. What brought you here?"

I learned that the coffee person used to work at the town's other hotel, which had recently closed for remodeling. "So after it's done, will you stay put or go back over there?" Mrs. Dunston asked. "Me, I have a son at the college, so that's what I'm doing, just checking in. He's my second boy, actually. The first one went here too. He's not working in his field yet, but with unemployment as high as it is, he's lucky to have anything at all. If I've told him that once, I've told him a hundred times, but, of course, being young, he's impatient, which is natural. Wants to set the world on fire, and if it can't happen by tomorrow morning at nine a.m., then life's just unfair and hardly worth living. What about you? Did you go to college?"

It's one thing to be jolly and talkative—my mother was that way. A dry cleaner, a gas-station attendant: no one behind a counter or cash register was spared the full force of her personality. The difference between her and Mrs. Dunston is that my mother had a sense of her audience—not just the person she was talking to but others around her who were listening in. "I can see you've got a line," she'd have said at some point, or, "Look at me, monopolizing all your time."

She'd also have made her chatter more compelling. In my mother's version, the underemployed son would sleep each day until dusk, possibly in a dank basement, with the leg of a dismembered child in his mouth. She spoke in a voice that addressed everyone and invited them to join in. Mrs. Dunston, on the other hand, was simply loud. Loud and just as dull as she could be.

After what felt like weeks, the young woman finished with the orders. Two cups the size of wastepaper baskets were placed upon the counter, and then Mr. Dunston reappeared and pointed out the plate-glass window toward a cluster of grim buildings on the other side of the parking lot. "What are those?" he asked.

The young woman said that they used to belong to the college. "Of course, that was before they expanded the west side of the campus."

"And when was that?" Mr. Dunston asked. He was a good ten years older than his wife, midsixties, maybe, and he wore a baseball cap with a tattered brim.

"I beg your pardon?" the young woman said.

"I said, when did they expand the west side of the campus? Was it recently or did they do it a long time ago?"

WHO THE HELL CARES? I wanted to shout. WHAT ARE YOU, THE OFFICIAL HISTORIAN OF WHO-GIVES-A-FUCK COLLEGE? DO YOU NOT NOTICE THAT THERE'S SOMEONE IN LINE BEHIND YOU? SOMEONE WHO'S BEEN STANDING HERE ROCKING BACK AND FORTH ON HIS GODDAMNED HEELS FOR THE LAST TEN MINUTES WHILE YOU AND THAT BRONTOSAURUS RUN YOUR STUPID MOUTHS ABOUT NOTHING?

I was this close to walking away, to marching off in a huff, but then Mrs. Dunston would have turned to her husband and the girl behind the counter, saying, "Some people!" I'd gotten a similar reaction the previous morning, when I'd squeezed past a couple standing side by side on the moving walkway connecting concourses A and B. "In a great big hurry to meet that heart attack!" the man had called after me.

I wanted to remind him that this was an airport and that some of us had a tight connection, if that was okay. But, of course, I had no connection, tight or otherwise. I just couldn't bear to see him and his wife standing side by side, blocking the way of someone who *might* have a tight connection.

The Dunstons' bill came to eight dollars, which, everyone agreed, *was* a lot to pay for two cups of coffee. But they *were* large ones, and this *was* a vacation, sort of. Not like a trip to Florida, but you certainly couldn't do that at the drop of a hat, especially with gas prices the way they are and looking to go even higher.

While talking, Mrs. Dunston rummaged through her tremendous purse. Her wallet was eventually located, but then it seemed that the register was locked, so the best solution was to put the coffees on her bill. That's how I discovered her name and her room number: 302.

My only question then was what time I should arrange her wake-up call for. *Let's see how chatty you feel at four a.m.,* I thought.

Then it was all about returning the wallet to the purse and getting that safely zipped up before taking her drink off the counter and starting in on her long good-bye.

When the two of them finally lumbered off toward the elevator, I approached the counter, hoping the woman behind it would roll her eyes, acknowledging that something really needed to be done about people like the Dunstons. She didn't, though, so I decided I would hate her as much as I'd hated them. When she told me that her little stand didn't serve regular brewed coffee, I hated her even more.

"I can do you a nice cappuccino," she said. "Or an iced latte, maybe?" This last word was delivered to my back as I stormed out the door. Then it was up the street and around the corner to a *real* coffee place. The pierced and tattooed staff members scowled at my approach, and I placed my order, confident that they would hate the Dunstons as much as, or possibly even more than, they already hated me.

Rubbish

I don't know why it is, exactly, but once Hugh and I settle in somewhere, we tend to stay put. All those years in France, and except for a single weekend in Arles, I never visited the lower half of the country. It was the same after our move to England. London, we knew, but everything outside it was a mystery to us, a sort of "out there" we planned to get to "one day." That day arrived in the summer of 2010, when we visited some friends in West Sussex. They'd told us the South Downs were beautiful, but we weren't prepared for just *how* beautiful; these massive, chalk-speckled hills so green they made our eyes cramp. The roads were narrow and bordered by trees that formed canopies overhead. All the houses had names, and that too seemed enchanting. Our friends live in what's called the Old Manor, which is near a place called the Granary. Hugh and I stayed with them for only one night, but it was enough to convince us, in the way that horrible, childless couples can be convinced of such things, that we needed to sell our vacation house in Normandy and resettle in West Sussex as soon as possible.

After returning to London we got on the Internet and found two properties that were within our price range. The first was called Faggotts Stack and was located between the hamlets of Balls Cross and Titty Hill. Sight unseen it had everything going for it. I'd have bought it just as a mailing address, but Hugh wanted something more beat-up, so we eventually went with choice number two, a cottage. Built, they reckoned, some four hundred years ago, it had no heat except for fireplaces and portable electric radiators. Half the windows wouldn't open, and the half that wouldn't close let in rain that rotted the floorboards and promoted great patches of mildew that clung like frost to the crumbling walls. There'd been a pig in the backyard but it had passed away—"Died of shame," Hugh guessed—that's how trashed the two-acre property was, a minefield of broken crockery, spent shotgun shells, and beer-bottle caps.

Slumped on the edge of it was the two-story cottage. Originally made of stone, it had been patched with brick and then patched again with what looked like dirty snowballs. The ground-floor windows had panes the size of tarot cards, and those were nice, as were the interior walls, which were crisscrossed with beams. The ceilings had them too, all corroded by worms and beetles.

"We'll take it," Hugh told me, this while standing in the living room, before we'd even seen the second floor. What with such a bucolic view—sheep grazing in the shadow of these great, verdant hills—

the work seemed inconsequential. "Give these people what they're asking, and do it today so we can get started."

If I had hesitated he would have left me. Because that's how Hugh is. You do not stand in his way; this I learned a long time ago. I also learned to trust him, especially in regard to property. Aside from the view, he liked that the place had not been modernized: none of the Sheetrocked closets or prefabricated shower stalls you'd just have to rip out and redo. Because the house was Grade II listed, broken windows could be replaced but not double-paned, as that would keep out the historic cold. Gutters and chimneys could be repaired, but you couldn't put skylights in the attic or even insulate the walls, as that would amount to smothering the original beams. Hugh asked if an interior kitchen door could be moved two feet to the left, and when the answer came it was not just "no" but something closer to "hell no." It's as though we had asked to have ice cubes in our wine, like, "Ick, who *are* you?"

We bought the house in late July and gave the previous owners three months to pack. I was out of the country when Hugh got the keys and the builders began what turned out to be a yearlong occupation. A lot of what they did was invisible. By this I mean drainage ditches and septic tanks. The ancient roof was taken off, and when it was put back on using the exact same lichen-covered tiles, it didn't look any different. Rotten floorboards were pried up, the mildew problem was seen to, and then the plumber and electrician arrived.

While the builders worked on the cottage, Hugh lived in what used to be the stable but was later converted into a guesthouse, the kind you'd have if you wanted to either discourage guests or contain them in one spot while slowly depressing them to death. It was especially grim in the winter, when in order to get warm you had to stand directly before the fireplace. There you'd rotate like a stump of gyro meat and wonder when the next train could carry you back to London.

By the time I finally joined Hugh in the stable, it was December, and I began to notice the many things that had escaped my attention on my previous visit. For instance, there's a gliding club a mile and a half away. On a website, its members rhapsodize about how peaceful it is. And they're right, gliders *are* quiet. The propeller planes that tow them into the sky, on the other hand, are like flying chain saws, and on a clear day their presence could be almost constant.

What really got to me, though, was all the rubbish on the sides of the road. In London the idea is that if you put something on a wall or stuff it between the slats of a fence, it doesn't count. Like it's only *really* litter if it touches the ground, at which point it's the wind that did it, not you. It's frustrating, but I'd grown to expect trash in a city. In the countryside, though, and in such beautiful countryside, it's heartbreaking, one of those things that, once you notice it, you can't stop noticing.

Our property faces a winding, tree-lined lane that leads to Amberley, a village so picturesque and meticulously cared for that it seems almost false, like a movie set. "You've got to be kidding me," I said the first time I saw it. Because it's almost too much: the cozy pub, the twelfth-century church, and the two dozen or so perfect cottages, many with sloping thatched roofs. The center of life is a little food shop, and walking to it on that first December afternoon, I saw more litter than I had the entire fifteen years I spent in Normandy. I said to a woman I passed along the way, "Did a parade just come through?"

When I mentioned the trash to the neighbors, they agreed that it was a disgrace. "It wasn't like this thirty years ago," said the woman in the house to the right of ours. She couldn't tell me why things had changed. It was just part of a general decline. In that regard it was like graffiti, something that had inexorably spread until people lost the will to fight against it. Then, to make themselves feel less powerless, they decided it was art. I tried looking at the trash that way: *Oh, how the light plays off that vodka bottle! Look at the bright blue candy wrapper, so vivid against the fallen brown leaves.* It didn't work, though.

On my second day at the house I got on my bike and rode to the town of Pulborough. The first few miles are on narrow roads cut through a magnificent forest, the floor of which is relatively free of underbrush. This makes it easier for the deer to run, and affords a clearer view of the trash, entire bags of it sometimes. These are sacks of household garbage that people feel inclined to abandon for one reason or another. They'll dump appliances too: microwaves, television sets, outdated sound systems released into the woods like they'd be happier there. There's a landfill these things could be taken to, but it costs money and you'd have to go out of your way, so why not feed it all to the foxes? They like stereos, don't they? And panini makers with frayed cords? Building supplies are another big item—cans of polyurethane, broken cinder blocks. Joint compound. Hot water heaters.

On the other side of the forest there's a busy two-lane road. I'd been riding on it for a quarter of a mile when I came upon a man collecting garbage into a plastic bag. He looked to be in his late forties and wore a stocking cap pulled low over his forehead. "Excuse me," I said, "but is someone paying you to do this?"

It was a wet day, and as a car barreled past, spraying me with mud, the man told me that he was acting on his own. "I live along here, and when the rubbish gets to be too much, when I just can't stand it anymore, I come out and collect it."

Another car sped by, and I said the queerest thing. "Well, you...," I told him, "you are just a...really good...citizen."

My face burned as I rode away, but later I'd reflect upon my goofy compliment and I would be glad that I'd stopped to offer it. It's not that I changed a life or anything, but as the weeks passed and I eventually *became* that man by the side of the road, I'd grow to understand the value of a little encouragement.

*   *   *

Pick up litter, and people assume that it's your punishment, part of your court-mandated community service. *Is it him who's been breaking into toolsheds?* they wonder. *Him who's been stealing batteries from parked cars?* At first I worried what passersby might think, but then my truer nature kicked in, and I became obsessed. When that happened there was no room for anyone else, except, occasionally, for Hugh, who does his part but won't pull the car over to collect every plastic bag he comes across. He can talk about litter, but when the topic shifts to the price of heating oil or the correct way to lay a paving stone, he can shift with it. For me, though, there is no other topic.

Here's who I've turned into since we moved to West Sussex: On a good day—a dry one—I don't have any mud on my clothes, just the usual dirt from crawling under fences, this to chase down empty bottles of Lucozade, an energy drink that gives its consumers the power to throw more bottles farther. My arms are scratched from reaching into blackberry bushes for empty potato chip bags, of which there are a never-ending supply, potato chips in the U.K. being like meals in space. "Argentinean Flame Grilled Steak" a bag will read, or the new "Cajun Squirrel."

Since cleaning roadsides has become my life, my fingertips have turned black, like spent matches, this the result of prying up bottle caps. There are almost always leaves and twigs in my hair, and because I know I'm going to get filthy, I dress for the occasion: in rags, like a hobo.

"You need to get yourself a good stick," one of my neighbors said. "The kind with a nail on the end. That'll save you from having to bend over."

It's a nice thought, but adding a harpoon to the mix would only make me more of an outcast. Then too, it might prove hard to carry. When I first started trash collecting, I did it on foot. Moving farther afield, I took to riding my bicycle, tying a bag of garbage to my rear fender and balancing a second, much larger one on my basket. On my back there's a knapsack with moist towelettes in it. These I need after picking up dirty diapers or packs of spoiled meat that maggots are living in. I say to myself, *Just leave it,* but if I did, the road wouldn't be clean, just *almost* clean, which is the same as fairly dirty.

Pedaling home through the forest, I'll peer over my full, teetering trash bag and review my efforts: not so much as a cigarette butt to spoil the view. *Enjoy it while you can,* I think, for by the next morning it will be defiled. Once, I found a stroller with the seat burned out, this as if the child had spontaneously combusted. Weeks later I came upon a sex magazine, but for the most part it's the same crap over and over, the crisp bags, the empty cans of beer and Red Bull, the endless Cadbury and Twix and Mars bars wrappers. The soda and candy point a finger toward kids, but according to the Campaign to Protect Rural England, one-quarter of the population readily admits to throwing trash out the window. That's thirteen million people I'm picking up after, and not one of them seems to appreciate it.

*   *   *

One afternoon while driving back from the beach, Hugh pointed out a McDonald's bag vomiting its contents onto the pavement. "I say that any company whose products are found on the ground automatically has to go out of business," he said. This is how we talk nowadays, as if our pronouncements hold actual weight and can be implemented at our discretion, like we're kings or warlocks. "That means no more McDonald's, no more Coke—none of it."

"That wouldn't affect you any," I told him. Hugh doesn't drink soda or eat Big Macs. "But what if it was something you needed, like paint? I find buckets of it in the woods all the time."

"Fine," he said. "Get rid of it. I'll make my own."

If anyone could make his own paint, it would be Hugh.

"What about brushes?"

"Please," he said, and he shifted into a higher gear. "I could make those in my sleep."

A few days later, returning from the butcher in Pulborough, he presented me with his goatskin-sack idea. "Everyone gets one, see. Then, if you want a soft drink or a takeaway coffee or whatever, that would be your mandatory container." He seemed so pleased with himself. "It could even have a strap on it," he said. "Like a canteen but soft."

"Well, wouldn't people just throw *those* out the window?"

"Too bad if they do, because they're only allowed one of them," he said.

"And how would you clean it?" I asked. "What if you wanted milk in the morning and wine at lunch? Wouldn't the flavors run into each other?"

"Just...shut up," he told me.

At night I lie in bed and map out the territory I'll cover the following day. The thing that holds me back is maintenance, retracing my steps and spot-cleaning the stretches of road I'd covered the previous afternoon and the afternoon before that. *What did my life consist of before this?* I wonder. *Surely there was something I was devoted to?*

With the arrival of warm weather, it became a bit easier to live in the stable. Three old friends visited from the United States, one in July and two more in August. "Want to pick up rubbish on the sides of the road?" I asked.

And all of them answered, "Sure. That sounds fun!"

I felt like the Horsham District Council should have given them something, a free tour of the Arundel Castle, maybe. It's the local government's responsibility to clear away the trash, but in order to maintain all the roads, they'd need a crew of hundreds. And until people change their behavior, how much can they actually accomplish?

"I'm not judging, but do you ever throw litter from your cars?" I asked the men working on our house. They all told me no, and I said, "Really, you can be honest with me."

I asked the cashier at the local shop, the owner

of the tearoom, the butcher. "No," they all told me. "Never."

I find a half-empty box of doughnuts and imagine it flung from the dimpled hand of a dieter, wailing, "Get this away from me." Perhaps the jumbo beer cans and empty bottles of booze are tossed for a similar reason. It's about denial, I tell myself, or, no, it's about anger, for isn't every piece of litter a way of saying "fuck you"?

In trying to make sense of it all, I create a weak-willed weight watcher, an alcoholic, an antisocial teenager, but the biggest litterer I ever knew was my Greek grandmother, who died in 1976. That woman would throw anything out a car window. Her only criteria was that it fit.

"What the hell are you doing?" my father used to shout, and it would take her a moment to figure out what he was referring to. *Farting? No. Throwing a paper grocery bag out onto the highway? What was wrong with that?* The important thing to Yiayiá wasn't a clean outside but a clean inside. A tidy station wagon reflected upon you personally, while a tidy landscape, what was that? Look at the sky, littered with clouds, or the beach trashed with shells. How was that mess any different from a hundred cans in a ditch?

My grandmother didn't drive, but if she had, there'd be no end to the garbage trail she might have left. It doesn't take many people to muck up a roadside. A devoted handful can do the trick. One of the things I find repeatedly is a plastic Diet Coke bottle containing a meticulously folded Mars bar wrapper. I imagine this is someone's after-work snack and that by putting the wrapper inside the empty bottle, the person feels he's done his bit. And though he *has* turned two pieces of trash into one, until he learns to keep it in his car, I don't think he's entitled to pat himself on the back. *Who are you?* I wondered the first and third and fifth time I came across one of these stuffed bottles. *Do you think about the four hundred years it will take for this to decompose, or is this as inconsequential to you as flushing a toilet?*

"What the government needs to do is take a sample of everyone's DNA," I said. "Then, when a bottle or can is discovered on the ground, we just run a test on the spout and throw the person in jail."

"What if they've poured it into a glass?" Hugh asked.

And I said, "Why do you have to make this so difficult?"

It's pathetic, really. Here we are, recent immigrants thinking that everything will be perfect once we fundamentally change the people who were actually born and raised here. I tell myself that it's possible sometimes, though deep down I suspect it's just rubbish.

Day In, Day Out

Seven is truly a wonderful age. For two days. That's the length of time my friend Pam and her son, Tyler, who is in the second grade, normally visit. He's at the stage where whatever I do, he wants to do. This includes wearing button-down shirts; singing "Galveston"—a song made popular by Glen Campbell—until everyone begs you to please, for the love of God, stop; and carrying a small Europa-brand reporter's notebook. I gave him one the last time he came to the house in West Sussex, and, aping me, he stuck it in his pocket alongside a pen. That afternoon Hugh drove us to the nearby town of Arundel to tour its castle. There was an issue of the local paper in the backseat of the car, and leafing through it on our way there, I came upon a headline that read, "Dangerous Olives Could Be on Sale."

"Hmm," I said, and I copied it into my little notebook.

Tyler did the same but with less conviction. "Why are we doing this again?"

"It's for your diary," I explained. "You jot things down during the day, then tomorrow morning you flesh them out."

"But why?" he asked. "What's the point?"

That's a question I've asked myself every day since September 5, 1977. I hadn't known on September 4 that the following afternoon I would start keeping a diary, or that it would consume me for the next thirty-five years and counting. It wasn't something I'd been putting off, but once I began, I knew that I had to keep doing it. I knew as well that what I was writing was not a journal but an old-fashioned, girlish, Keep-Out-This-Means-You diary. Often the terms are used interchangeably, though I've never understood why. Both have the word "day" at their root, but a journal, in my opinion, is a repository of ideas—your brain on the page. A diary, by contrast, is your heart. As for "journal*ing*," a verb that cropped up at around the same time as "scrapbook-ing," that just means you're spooky and have way too much time on your hands.

A few things have changed since that first entry in 1977, but I've never wavered in my devotion, skip-ping, on average, maybe one or two days a year. It's not that I think my life is important or that future generations might care to know that on June 6, 2009, a woman with a deaf, drug-addicted mother-in-law taught me to say "I need you to stop being an asshole" in sign language. Perhaps it just feeds into my compulsive nature, the need to do the exact same thing at the exact same time every morn-ing. Some diary sessions are longer than others, but the length has more to do with my mood than with what's been going on. I met Gene Hackman once and wrote three hundred words about it. Six weeks later I watched a centipede attack and kill a worm and filled two pages. And I really *like* Gene Hackman.

In the beginning I wrote my diary on the backs of paper place mats. My friend Ronnie and I were hitch-hiking up the West Coast at the time. I was mailing regular letters and postcards to my friends back home, but because I had no fixed address, no one could answer them. And so I began writing to myself. Those first several years are hard to reread, not because they're boring—a diary is fully licensed to be boring—but because the writing is so horribly affected. It's poetry written by someone who's never read any poetry but seems to think its key is

   lowercase letters
   and lots of
    empty
      spaces.

I'd love to know how much it cost me to do a load of laundry—something, *anything* practical—but instead it's all gibberish. I was living in places without locks on the doors, and perhaps I worried that if someone found my diary and discovered what I was actually like, they'd dismiss me as dull and middle-class, far from the artist I was making myself out to be. So instead of recounting my first day of work at the Carolina Coffee Shop, I wrote, "I did not see *Star Wars*," one hundred times in red pen.

After a few months of place mats, I switched to hardcover sketchbooks and began gluing things around my entries: rent receipts, ticket stubs—ephemera that ultimately tell me much more than the writing does. Then came an embarrassing drawing phase, which was followed by a slightly less embarrassing collage jag. In 1979, I began typing my diaries, jerkily, with one finger, and having the pages bound between hand-painted cardboard covers. This meant that rather than writing publicly, most often in pancake houses, sometimes with a beret atop my head, I did it at home, in a real apartment now, with a lock on the door.

Perhaps it was this—the privacy—that allowed me to relax and settle into myself. In June of that year, I wrote that gas in four states had reached a dollar a gallon—"A dollar!" I wrote that after our German shepherd, Mädchen II, peed on my parents' bed, my mother entered a new dimension of cursing by calling the dog, who was female, a "shitty motherfucker." Finally I was recording my world and writing down things that seemed worth remembering. Then I discovered crystal meth and took two giant steps backward. The following six diaries amount to one jittery run-on sentence, a fever dream as humorless as it is self-important. I tried rereading it recently and came away wondering, *Who is this exhausting drug addict?*

I wanted to deny him, but that's the terrible power of a diary: it not only calls forth the person you used to be but rubs your nose in him, reminding you that not all change is evolutionary. More often than not, you didn't learn from your mistakes. You didn't get wiser but simply older, growing from the twenty-five-year-old who got stoned and accidentally peed on his friend Katherine's kitten to the thirty-five-year-old who got drunk and peed in the sandbox at his old elementary school. "The sandbox!" my sister Amy said at the time. "Don't you realize that *children* have to pee in there?"

My diary regained its footing after I gave up speed. Writing-wise it was still clumsy, but at least the focus widened. I didn't own a TV at the time but wrote a lot about the radio I was listening to. Occasionally I'd tune in to a music station, but I always preferred the sound of people talking, even if the subject was something I didn't care about—sports, for instance, or the likelihood of Jesus returning within the next few hours.

Radio played a bigger role in my diary when I moved to Chicago in 1984 and started listening to a weekly Sunday-night program called *Getting Personal*, hosted by a woman named Phyllis Levy. It's easy to hear a sex therapist today, but this was not a podcast or a satellite program where you could use whatever language you wanted to. Phyllis Levy was on a commercial station. Both she and her callers had to watch their mouths, thus using words like "pleasuring" and "cavity," which somehow sound much dirtier than their more common alternatives.

I often wrote about how understanding this woman was, how accepting. The only time I recall her drawing the line was when a man wanted to have sex in his half-blind wife's empty eye socket. Looking back, I think it must have been a joke. I mean, really, who does things like that? Phyllis, to her credit, took the call seriously, gently suggesting that with the wealth of other holes nature has provided us, perhaps this particular one was best left unexplored. Coming from North Carolina, I couldn't believe that this was on the radio. And on a Sunday! I used to listen at the typewriter and copy down the questions and answers I found most compelling. Other people's sex lives were great fun to write about. When it came to my own, however, I couldn't have been more discreet. Early diaries mention that "B. came over and spent the night" or that "After dinner M. and I were romantic twice." There are no details, much less full names. I think I worried that if someone ever read what I had written, the sex would be more embarrassing than, what, exactly? The whining about *not* having sex?

While a student in Chicago, my worst fear was realized when someone I'd been seriously dating got his hands on my diary. I was out of town at the time, and later learned that he was hurt, not by what I'd written about him but by his almost complete absence. I'd actually devoted more space to my barber than I had to him, and of course to the goings-on at school. At the start of my second year, I signed up for a creative-writing class. The instructor, a woman named Lynn, demanded that we each keep a journal and that we surrender it twice during the course of the semester. This meant that I'd be writing two diaries, one for myself and a second, heavily edited one, for her.

The entries I ultimately handed in are the sorts I read onstage sometimes, the .01 percent that might possibly qualify as entertaining: a joke I heard, a T-shirt slogan, a bit of inside information passed on by a waitress or cabdriver. To find these things, I turn to my diary index, which leaves out all the mumbly stuff and lists only items that might come in handy someday.

Volume 87, 5/15: Lisa puts a used Kotex through the wash, and her husband mistakes it for a shoulder pad.

Volume 128, 1/23: Told by saleswoman that the coat I'm trying on is waterproof "if it only rains a little."

Volume 129, 4/6: I write down my e-mail address for Ian, and after looking at it he says, "Oh my God. You have handwriting just like Hitler's." Note: what kind of person knows what Hitler's handwriting looks like?

Volume 132, 12/5: Sister Gretchen has her furnace serviced by a man named Mike Hunt.

Over a given three-month period, there may be fifty bits worth noting, and six that, with a little work, I might consider reading out loud. Leafing through the index, which now numbers 280 pages, I note how my entries have changed over the years, becoming less reflective and more sketchlike. It's five a.m. in the lobby of the La Valencia Hotel, and two employees are discussing parental advice. "I tell my sons they should always hold the door open for a woman," says the desk clerk. He is a Hispanic man, portly, with a lot of silver in his mouth. A second man stands not far away, putting newspapers into bags, and he nods in agreement. "I tell them it doesn't matter who the lady is. It could be a fat chick, but on the other side of the room, a pretty one might look over and notice, so even then it's not wasted."

Here is a passenger on the Eurostar from Paris to London, an American woman in a sand-colored vest hitting her teenage granddaughter with a guidebook until the girl cries. "You are a very lazy, very selfish person," she scolds. "Nothing like your sister."

If I sit down six months or a year or five years from now and decide to put this into an essay, I'll no doubt berate myself for not adding more details. What sort of shoes was the granddaughter wearing? What was the name of the book the old woman was hitting her with? But if you added every detail of everything that struck you as curious or spectacular, you'd have no time for anything else. As it is, I seem to be pushing it. Hugh and I will go on a trip, and while he's out, walking the streets of Manila or Reykjavík or wherever we happen to be, I'm back at the hotel, writing about an argument we'd overheard in the breakfast room. It's not lost on me that I'm so busy recording life, I don't have time to really live it. I've become like one of those people I hate, the sort who go to the museum and, instead of looking at the magnificent Brueghel, take a picture of it, reducing it from art to proof. It's not "Look what Brueghel did, painted this masterpiece" but "Look what *I* did, went to Rotterdam and stood in front of a Brueghel painting!"

Were I to leave the hotel *without* writing in my diary, though, I'd feel too antsy and incomplete to enjoy myself. Even if what I'm recording is of no consequence, I've got to put it down on paper.

"I think that what you have is a disorder," Hugh likes to say. But who proves invaluable when he wants the name of that restaurant in Barcelona that served the Camembert ice cream? The brand of soap his mother likes? The punch line of that joke he never thought was funny? "Oh, you remember. Something about a woman donating plasma," he says.

Of course, the diary helps me as well. "That certainly wasn't your position on July 7, 1991," I'll remind Hugh an hour after we've had a fight. I'd have loved to rebut him sooner, but it takes a while to look these things up.

The diary also comes in handy with my family, though there it plays the same role as a long-lost photograph. "Remember that time in Greece when I fell asleep on the bus and you coated my eyelids with toothpaste?" I'll say to my brother, Paul.

To heavy pot smokers, reminders like these are a revelation. "Wait a minute, we went to Greece?"

As a child I assumed that when I reached adulthood, I would have grown-up thoughts. By this I meant that I would stop living in a fantasy world;

that, while standing in line for a hamburger or my shot at the ATM, I would not daydream about befriending a gorilla or inventing a pill that would make hair waterproof. In this regard too, my diaries have proven me wrong. All I do is think up impossible situations: here I am milking a panda, then performing surgery, then clearing the state of Arizona with a tidal wave. In late November 2011, my most lurid fantasies involved catching the person who'd stolen my computer, the one I hadn't backed up in almost a year. I'd printed out my diary through September 21, but the eight weeks that followed were gone forever. "Two months of my life, erased!" I said to Hugh.

He reminded me that I had actually lived those two months. "The *time* wasn't stolen," he said, "just your record of it." This was a distinction that, after thirty-four years of diary keeping, I was no longer able to recognize. Fortunately I still had my notebooks, and as soon as the police left, I bought a new laptop and sat down to recover my missing eight weeks.

The first challenge was reading my handwriting, and the second was determining what the notes referred to. After making out "shaved stranger," I thought for a while and recalled a woman in the Dallas airport. We were waiting to board a flight to San Antonio, and I overheard her talking about her cat. It was long-haired, a male, I think, and she had returned home one day the previous summer to find that he had been shaved.

"Well, in that heat it was probably for the best," the man she was talking to said.

"But it wasn't *me* who shaved it," the woman said. "It was somebody else!"

"A stranger shaved your cat?"

"That's what I've been trying to tell you!" the woman said.

I eventually re-created the missing two months, printed them out, and placed the finished diary in my locked cabinet beside the 136 others that are shelved there.

"What should I do with these things when you die?" Hugh asks.

The way I see it, my options are burial or cremation. "But save the covers," I tell him. "The covers are nice."

As for seven-year-old Tyler, who knows if he'll stick with it? A child's diary, like a child's drawing of a house, is a fairly simple affair. "We went to a castle. It was fun. Then we went to a little zoo. That was fun too."

I thought my account of August 11 would begin with an accident I'd had at the castle. We were in the formal gardens when I took a wrong step and fell down before a great number of people, one of whom shouted—making me feel not just stupid but stupid *and* old—"Don't move him!"

My face burned as I picked myself up off the ground.

"That happened to me not long ago," Pam said, trying to make me feel better.

"It's what you get for horsing around," Hugh scolded.

Tyler said simply and honestly, "That was really funny."

I pulled out my notebook and wrote—as if I would possibly forget about it by the following morning when I'd limp to my desk—"Fell down in garden." I was mentally writing the diary entry, the embarrassment I felt, the stabbing pain in my knee, the sound of my body skidding on the gravel path, when we entered the castle's petting zoo and I saw something that moved my fall from the front page to the category of "other news." The place wasn't much: some chickens, a family of meerkats, a pony or two. In one large cage lived a pair of ferrets and, next door, some long-haired guinea pigs. A woman and her two sons, aged maybe five and seven, spotted them at the same time I did and raced over to get a better look. The younger boy seemed pleased enough, but his brother went bananas. "Jesus!" he said, turning to look at his mother. "Jesus, will you look at those?"

I pulled out my notebook.

"What are you writing down?" Tyler asked.

"Have you ever *seen* guinea pigs so big?" the boy asked. "I mean, *Jesus!*"

The woman offered Tyler and me an embarrassed look. "You shouldn't use the Lord's name like that, Jerry. Some people might find it offensive."

"Christ Almighty," the kid continued. "Someone should take a picture."

Writing about it the following morning, I'd recall how incredulous the boy had sounded. Yes, the guinea pigs were big—like furry slippers, sizes nine and ten and a half. They were hardly gargantuan, though. Had he possibly confused them with hamsters? The look on his face and his unexpected reaction—evoking Jesus as a weather-beaten adult would—were remarkable to me, and standing there in that dinky zoo, my knee throbbing, my little notebook firmly in hand, I knew I needed to keep the moment forever.

Mind the Gap

I said to my father yesterday afternoon, "Do you fancy my new jumper?"

When he answered, "Huh?" I was like, "'Jumper?' It means 'sweater' in England."

"Right," he said, adding that it was ninety-two degrees out and that if I didn't take it off I was guaranteed to get heatstroke or at least a rash, and wasn't that the last thing either of us needed at a time like this?

"Ninety-two degrees or not, I still think it's the most brilliant jumper I've ever seen," I told him.

My father made some joke about giving it an IQ test, but honestly, by that point, I'd stopped listening. We were in the driveway at the time. He was watering his dried-out hydrangeas, and I was sitting on the bonnet of the car, just waiting for him to call it the hood or some such thing. He's so stupid, my father is. My mum wasn't much brighter, but now that she's dead I'm just trying to concentrate on the good things, like how she paid for me to go to England with my school's history club. I'm not a member—it's actually one of my worst subjects—but the adviser, Mrs. Carkeek, let me come anyway because she needed a minimum of twelve students and only had eleven after Kimberly Shank got a B in German and tried to kill herself. It was my first time out of the country, and it really opened my eyes to what stupid cunts the people are here in the United States.

"How can I be a cunt when I'm a guy?" Braydon Hoyt asked when I saw him at the funeral on Tuesday. He didn't know that the word means "idiot," so the more times he asked, the more of a cunt he became. (And to think I once dated him!!!) The problem with Braydon, and with all American blokes, really, is that they're so literal. And it's not just me who thinks that way. Fiona, who's my best mate in England, said that except for me she won't go anywhere *near* an American because they don't know what irony is. She and I met outside the Globe. Mrs. Carkeek had taken the group to see *The Temptress,* I think it was, but the play was so bloody boring I snuck out at intermission. In front of the theater is a walkway that faces the river, and that's where I met Fiona. "Fag?" she asked.

That's how I got practically addicted to Mayfairs, which, unfortunately, you can't get in the States. I ask everywhere, and people look at me like I'm crazy. "Blue box? Big picture of a diseased lung on it?" You can't find Walkers Prawn Cocktail crisps here either, which is another thing Fiona turned me on to. She and I talked for almost ten minutes before she realized I wasn't English. "Wait a minute," she said. "*You're* a Yank? Really? *You?*"

At first she was thrown by the way I talk. I don't notice it myself, but according to Dad and everyone at the funeral, I completely picked up an English accent during the week I spent there. "It's not just that though," Fiona said. "It's your Union Jack jumper, your Doc Martens, your whole way of being."

By this she meant my attitude—the way I can look at something and automatically see that it's complete bollocks. Fiona has that same ability, and we agreed that it's a double-edged sword. "I mean, sometimes, McKenzie, don't you look at all these stupid gits and just wish you could be that easily satisfied?"

It was crazy how much the two of us had in common. Both of us love London, for a start. She wasn't born there but moved from Coventry when she was fifteen to live with her granny in Barking. I think "granny" is absolutely the most brilliant thing ever to call your grandmother, but unfortunately it doesn't work in the United States. My mum's mother just wants me to call her T.J. "I'm sixty-two years old, for God's sake," she said on Tuesday when I saw her at the funeral. "I'm young and I'm active, and if you ever call me that again, I'll wash your mouth out with soap." I've never seen her so mad. "And don't tell me that in England the soap is called 'chuff' or something, or I'll wash it out twice."

My other grandmother—the one on my dad's side—had a stroke last winter, so I honestly don't know what she said when I called her granny, but she didn't look too happy about it. She's out of her wheelchair finally, but if it were up to me, I'd put her back in it. My God, was she slow—took her twenty minutes to get from our sofa to the loo. That means "bathroom" in England. Our ground-floor loo has an old person's bar next to the toilet. Dad put it in at Easter when Mum got really bad, and I told him I'm not going back in there until he takes it out again.

"Why?" he asked.

"It makes me feel like I'm in hospital," I told him.

"In *a* hospital, you mean," he said.

Six days earlier I'd had the same conversation, but in the other direction.

"My mother's been in the hospital for almost three weeks now," I'd said to Fiona.

And she said, "'*In* hospital.' We leave out the 'the' here." She offered me another Mayfair. "So what's she in for?"

"Cancer of ovaries," I told her.

The Globe was on a Thursday. On Friday we took a day trip to Oxford, which the history club wankers practically wet themselves over, and just as we returned to London, at half six English time but twelve thirty in Missouri, my mother died. We were scheduled to fly home on Saturday, so rather than ruin the rest of my trip, my dad didn't tell me until we saw each other at the airport. I actually can't stand anyone in the history club so didn't really mind that they saw my stupid father weeping like a girl at the baggage claim. I said to him later in the car, "Do you have to be so *American* about this? I mean, really. It's not like you didn't know it was coming."

Something Fiona had noticed and I completely agree with is that people in the States are entirely too sentimental. They really will cry at the drop of a hat, partly because they're babies and partly because they're too attached to things. Not me, though. "Keep calm and carry on," that's my motto. I bought a mug that says so, and it's absolutely the only thing I'll drink my tea out of. I'm mad for tea.

Due to the jet lag, I was knackered out of my mind for the funeral. Not that it mattered, really. Like I wrote to Fiona, it was absolute rubbish. There I was, *dying* for a Mayfair, while all these people who hardly even knew my mother came up to say how much they were going to miss her. If I had a dime for every time I heard "Look how big you've gotten!" I'd have enough for a first-class ticket back to London *and* a whole year's rent on a flat. *Two* years' rent if I shared it with a flatmate.

After the funeral, scores of perfectly dreadful people came by the house. Luckily my grandmothers were there to help. Well, *one* was a help, the other just sat there like a toad and blinked. I only had a few chances to slip away, and when I did I went to my room and checked to see if I'd gotten any e-mails. I've written Fiona eighteen times since returning home but haven't heard anything back quite yet, probably because she's uncomfortable. English people are completely different than we are, especially about money. While Americans are all "Look what I've got!" the Brits are a lot more British about it, a lot more stoical and private. It wasn't easy for Fiona to ask me for that loan. The whole subject was a complete embarrassment for her, I could tell. Especially given that she was so much older than me, in her thirties at least, not that that makes any difference. Due to my maturity, I have all kinds of older friends, or could if I wanted to. Fiona walked me to three different ATMs in order to get the money— so while the history club was at the Globe, being tourists, I was seeing the *real* London and falling desperately in love with it.

I was hoping that after graduation two years from now I could go to college there, but it turns out I'm already in college. Brits call high school "college," and what we call college they call "uni." Fiona says it's strictly for gits and arseholes, but at least it would be a foot in the door. My father won't like the idea one bit, but he'd better start getting used to it. He's too preoccupied to realize it now, but in a lot of ways, I'm already gone.

A Cold Case

There are plenty of things I take for granted, but not being burglarized was never one of them. Whether I was in a good neighborhood or a crummy one, in a house or apartment or hotel room, every time I walked in and found my dresser drawers not emptied onto the floor, I would offer a silent, nondenominational prayer of thanks. I honestly believed that my gratitude would keep me safe, so imagine my surprise in late November 2011, when someone broke into a place I was renting with Hugh and my sister Gretchen and stole my computer bag.

I thought of my laptop—a year's worth of work, gone!—but my real concern was my passport, which had been tucked into an interior pocket alongside my checkbook. Its loss was colossal because it was my only form of ID, and also because my Indefinite Leave to Remain sticker was in it.

This is the British equivalent of a green card, and getting it had not been easy. Before Indefinite Leave I'd had visas, and those had taken some effort as well. The rules have changed since I first applied, but in 2002 it was possible to qualify as a writer. All I had to do was fill out a great many forms and prove that I had published a book. Hugh, by extension, was granted a visa as the boyfriend of a writer. This meant that when crossing into England, I would be asked by the border agents if I wrote mysteries, and Hugh would be asked if his boyfriend wrote mysteries. No other genre was ever considered.

We had to renew our visas every few years. This involved going to the dismal town of Croydon and spending a day in what was always the longest and most desperate line I had ever imagined. It was also the most diverse. I thought I was good at identifying languages, but it turns out I know next to nothing. *Surely they're making that up,* I'd think, listening in on the couple ahead of me. The woman, most often, would be dressed like the grim reaper. Her husband would wear a sweatshirt with a picture of a boat or a horse on it, and the two would be speaking something so unmelodious and dire-sounding I could not imagine it having the words for "birthday cake." If Hugh and I were denied extensions of our visas, we would have returned to Paris or New York, while they'd have gone back to, what? Beheadings? Clitoridectomies? What they had at stake was life-and-death. What we had at stake was Yorkshire pudding.

The nuisance of visas and having them renewed was something I left to Hugh, who's a whiz at that sort of thing. There was nothing the authorities demanded that he couldn't locate: our original birth certificates, a hank of his grandmother's hair, the shoes I wore when I was twelve. People think it's easy to leave home and resettle in another country, but in fact it's exhausting, and purposefully so. The government's hope is to weed out the lazy, though all it really eliminates are those who can't afford an immigration lawyer. Had we not been native English speakers, and had Hugh not loved the challenges, we'd have hired one as well. As it was, we renewed our visas the requisite three times and then applied for Indefinite Leave. Aside from the mountain of paperwork, this involved reading a manual called *Life in the UK* and taking a subsequent test.

Hugh sat for it on the same day I did, and we spent weeks in the summer of 2008 studying. During that time I learned the difference between the House of Lords and the House of Commons. I learned that in 1857 British women won the right to divorce their husbands. I learned that people below the age of sixteen cannot deliver milk in the U.K., but I don't think I learned why. It was just one of those weird English injustices, like summer.

Before taking the real test, I took the fake ones provided at the back of the study manual. "What do people eat on Christmas?" was one of the questions. Another was "What do you do on Halloween when someone comes to the door?" It was multiple-choice, and possible answers included "call the police" and "run and hide."

I laughed, but these weren't jokes. If you were from Chad, you'd likely freak out when children with panty hose over their heads showed up at your house demanding that you give them candy. As for the Christmas-meal question, do I know what they eat in Nigeria for Eid-el-Kabir or in Beijing for Qing-ming?

Another of the test questions asked why great numbers of Jewish people immigrated to the U.K. in the early part of the twentieth century. I don't recall all the possible answers, but A was "to escape racist attacks" and C was "to invade and seize land."

Hugh and I took our tests along with a dozen other foreigners, and though they didn't give us our grades, I'm pretty sure I had a perfect score. He missed a question about the cost of eye exams for people over sixty but otherwise got everything right. Our Indefinite Leave stickers were nothing much to look at—just our pictures surrounded by stamps and seals—but still we gazed at them for hours on end, the way you might at a picture of the baby you birthed upside down in a burning house after a difficult seven-year pregnancy. While juggling knives.

The next step is to get our British passports, though it's not necessary. As it is, Hugh and I can live and work in the U.K. for the rest of our lives.

I had my Indefinite Leave for four years before my passport was stolen. The theft took place on Oahu. Telling people this erases the sympathy I get for being burglarized, so I'm always inclined to leave it out. Then too, there seems nothing specifically Hawaiian about it. There are only two places to get robbed:

TV and the real world. On television you get your stuff back. In the real world, if you're lucky, the policeman who responds to your call will wonder what kind of computer it was. Don't let this get your hopes up. Chances are he's asking only because he has a software question. The officer who responded to our call was prompt but not terribly reassuring. "Yeah"—she sighed, looking at the spot where my stolen property used to be—"we get a lot of burgs in this area."

That's how lazy she was—couldn't even squeeze out the extra two syllables.

There was an oceanfront park a quarter of a mile up the road from our rental house, so after the police left I walked over with Gretchen, convinced that in one of the trash cans I would discover my computer bag. The laptop would be gone, I figured, but surely I would find my passport. It's crazy how certain I was. Gretchen and I looked in one trash can after another, and just as I started searching the bushes, I realized how big the world is. You'd think I might have noticed this before, perhaps while on a twenty-three-hour flight from London to Sydney, but the size of a planet doesn't really strike you until you start looking for something. It could have been anywhere, my old passport, but in my mind's eye I saw it on a scratched-up, glass-topped coffee table, the surface of which was dusted with meth.

I suppose the people who steal from us could be decent and well intentioned. The things they take while we're out working—our watches and cameras, the wedding rings passed down by our great-grand-

mothers—they're all going to feed a sick child or
to buy a new hip for a colorful and deserving old
person. That, though, would make things too complicated. Much simpler to do like I did, and decide
that these people are scum. Your stuff was sold off
for a bag of dope, and while you lie awake, turning
it over in your mind, your thief is getting high somewhere in front of a stolen TV. Remorse? His only
regrets are that you weren't away from home longer
and that you didn't have better things.

I have it on good authority that in the days before
DNA testing, a great many burglars used to shit
on their victims' beds or carpets—this as an added
insult before heading back out the window or whichever hole they'd crept in through. That they could
defecate on command like that, and solely for spite,
further illustrated their depravity in my book.

My computer was stolen at eleven o'clock on a
Tuesday morning, and that night I had a reading in
Honolulu. Several stars from the crime series *Hawaii
Five-O* came backstage before the show and were in-
finitely more helpful than the real police officers I'd
dealt with earlier in the day. "The first thing we need
to do is set up a reward," said the actor who played
Detective Lieutenant Chin Ho Kelly. I'd never spoken to anyone so handsome, and said in response,
obviously dazed, "You'll be my what?"

Hugh, Gretchen, and I stayed on Oahu for another
five days, and afterward, with me using my police report as ID, we flew to Los Angeles, where I secured

a new passport. The picture in my stolen one wasn't half bad, but in the new one I look like a penis with an old person's face drawn on it. I could have had more photos taken, but it wouldn't have made any difference. This was the new me, post-theft—all my youthful optimism gone, filched by some drug addict in Hawaii. Every time I looked at my horrible new passport, I thought of him and wondered what he was up to. The person I pictured was in his mid-to-late twenties, with a vibrant tattoo on his neck—something classy, perhaps a scorpion waving a joint. He was like a paper doll I would accessorize with whatever I found irritating that day: He texted during movies. He ate at Chick-fil-A. He put glitter in his thank-you letters, and when you opened them the damn stuff got all over everything.

I often wondered if my thief had ever been caught. If he'd spent time in jail, who had bailed him out? His mother? His girlfriend? I figured he was straight, since a gay person, or even a bisexual, would have also taken my rubberized canvas tote, which was right next to my computer bag and which prompts compliments like you would not believe.

In early December 2011 I flew back to London. Border agents in France don't care who comes into their country, but in England it's a different story. "What are you doing here?" they want to know. "What are you *really* doing here?" Indefinite Leave put an end to these questions, but now, without it, I was back to square one, treated like a lowly visitor.

"How long will you be in the U.K.?" asked my Heathrow border agent. "Where are you staying?"

I explained my situation, and after asking me to step to the side, the man carried my passport into an office and looked me up on the computer. It confirmed my Indefinite Leave, and I was free to go. No problem. Returning from South Korea a month later, I had the exact same experience. Then I took the train to Paris, and on my return I got a female border agent who really laid into me. "Why haven't you gotten a new Indefinite Leave sticker?"

I reminded her that the process takes a great deal of time. It involves surrendering your passport—a problem, as I'd been traveling nonstop for work.

She crossed her arms. "What do you do for a living?"

I told her I was a writer, and she said very sternly that I could write at home.

"Well, not about *South Korea*," I wanted to say, but it's pointless to argue with people like her, so I just stood there, shaking.

"I don't even have to let you in," she hissed. "Do you realize that?"

I cleared my throat. "Yes."

"What did you say?"

I felt the people behind me watching, and sensed them thinking, as I often do, *What's with the troublemaker?* "Yes."

"Yes, what?"

It seemed she wouldn't be happy until I was crying. "Yes, I realize you don't have to let me in."

I don't think I've ever felt more foolish than I did

at that moment. Who was I to feel at home in another country, to believe that filling out forms and scoring high marks on a test guaranteed me the same sense of belonging I take for granted in the United States? Had a border agent *there* given me trouble, I might have gotten frustrated, but I doubt that my hands would have shaken, or that my voice, after climbing another three octaves, would have quivered and broken, leaving me to sound like Snow White with Parkinson's. "But...," I wanted to say, "but I thought you *liked* me."

"Walk this way." The woman lifted herself, muttering, from her chair, and as she left her booth, I glanced at her belt, expecting to find scalps swinging from it. Grabbing my bag, I followed her to an office, where one of her colleagues looked me up on the computer. My passport was stamped, and after ten minutes spent sitting on a bench and thinking about my thief, I was free to go. Hugh suggested I'd simply gotten the wrong border agent, but the experience was so unsettling that after returning to London I had him complete the paperwork for a new Indefinite Leave sticker. The forms were sent, along with my passport and a sizable check, to the British Home Office, and after a week I received a letter saying that they'd gotten my envelope and should hopefully get back to me within six months.

I said to Hugh, "*Six* months?"

"That's at the latest," he told me. "For all you know, it could come next week."

*   *   *

I sent off my passport at the beginning of June, and when, by mid-July, it had still not been returned, I had to cancel a reading in Italy. When it did not come by the end of July, I had to forfeit a nonrefundable Eurostar ticket to France. Nobody likes having a problem, but having a convoluted, bureaucratic one is even more galling. When I explained it to people face-to-face, I would see their eyes glazing over, and when I explained it over the phone, I could feel them turning on their computers and checking their retirement accounts.

Without my passport, I was stuck in the country I had immigrated to. And all because of some drug addict in Hawaii. While he got high on the beach, I endured one of the wettest, coldest summers on record. Growing up in North Carolina, I got my fill of hot, sticky weather. Ninety-degree heat does nothing for me—I hate it. A little warmth wouldn't have hurt, though, a couple of days when I didn't have to wear both a sweater *and* a long undershirt, these beneath a hideous plastic poncho. I honestly hadn't known it was possible to rain that much. It was so bad in West Sussex that baby birds were drowning in their nests. Even frogs were dying. Frogs! Our Italy trip was to be a reading with a few days of vacation tacked on. But instead of driving through the Piedmont with Hugh and our friend Eduardo, I walked the roads surrounding our house, wearing knee-high Wellingtons and watching as bloated slugs floated by.

Everyone but me seemed to be going places.

Once a week, in an attempt to break the

monotony, Hugh and I would grab our jumbo golf umbrellas and slog down the road to the pub, where we'd catch up on the local news. One of our few neighbors who had not yet flown to Spain had her house broken into while she was upstairs asleep. The thief stole her purse and, after discovering that her car keys were in it, took her Audi as well. In response, the local police suggested that, as a precautionary measure, we all start sleeping with our keys.

Had they responded this way in France or America, it wouldn't have surprised me, but wasn't everyone in England supposed to be a detective? Wasn't every crime, no matter how complex, solved in a timely fashion by either a professional or a hobbyist? That's the impression you get from British books and TV shows. Sherlock Holmes, Miss Marple, Hetty Wainthropp, Inspector George Gently: they come from every class and corner of the country. There's even Edith Pargeter's Brother Cadfael, a Benedictine monk who solved crimes in twelfth-century Shrewsbury. No surveillance cameras, no fingerprints, not even a telephone, and still he cracked every case that came his way. But now, almost nine hundred years later, the solution is *to sleep with our keys?* "How's that for progress?" I said to Hugh as we waded home. "I mean, why not just tell us to sleep in our cars?"

In mid-October I was scheduled to fly to the U.S., and then on to thirty cities as part of a lecture tour. Canceling it was out of the question, so in early

September I called the Home Office and demanded that they send my passport back. This meant canceling my application and losing the five hundred dollars that accompanied it, but what choice did I have? The person I spoke to on the phone explained that the return process could take up to twenty working days. She also said that if I left for the States, there was no guarantee the British government would let me back into the U.K.

I hung up thinking there were worse things than being deported from England. What's with a country that takes six months to replace a sticker in somebody's passport, this when it's all right there on the computer? Then I thought of other things I don't like about the place: the littering, the public drunkenness, the way they say "Jan" instead of January. There are problems everywhere, of course. It's just that without my passport I can't adequately appreciate them.

A few days into my tour of the U.S., someone on Oahu came upon a computer bag with a checkbook and a passport in it. He or she then took them to the nearest post office, along with a note reading, "Aloha. These were found abandoned. Very important documents. I hope they can find their way back to the owner." There was no name at the bottom, just the word "Thanks."

The postal supervisor used my checkbook to track down my banker, and three days later I had my old passport back. After opening it up and kissing my Indefinite Leave to Remain sticker, I called the Hawaiian postal supervisor, who told me that my things had been found in the vicinity of the house I'd rented, not far from the area I'd scoured with Gretchen. That was all he could tell me. Neither the passport nor the checkbook smelled of mildew, so maybe they were only recently tossed out. By whom? I no longer care. Instead of thinking about my burglar, I'm turning my imagination toward the unidentified person who so thoughtfully ended my nightmare with the British Home Office. I think of good instead of evil. I believe in luck again. It would have been nice to get my computer back, but I can live with its loss. My only regret is that my case was so anticlimactic. What began as a mystery ended as an even bigger one. *Who are you, Good Samaritan?* I wonder. *What are you doing right this minute? Donating bone marrow? Reading to the blind? Teaching crippled children to dance?*

On returning to England in early December, I handed two passports to my Heathrow border agent. He looked at the old one containing my Indefinite Leave sticker, and then at the new one, which he stamped and handed back. He may have said, "Welcome home," or it might have been simply "Next." In the way of people who have better things on their minds, I didn't quite bother to listen.

The Happy Place

It was late September, and Hugh and I were in Amsterdam. We'd been invited out for dinner, so at five o'clock we left our hotel and took an alarming one-hundred-twenty-dollar cab ride to the home of our hostess, a children's book author who lived beside a canal in the middle of nowhere. By the time we arrived, it was dark. Someone opened the door to greet us, and it took me a moment to realize it was Francine. Obscuring her face were two clear plastic bags filled with water. Both were suspended by strings, just sort of sagging there, like testicles. I, of course, asked about them, and she said they were for keeping the flies away. "I don't know what it is, but they see or sense these sandwich bags and immediately head off in another direction. Isn't that right, Pauline?" Francine said to her girlfriend. "Not one fly all summer, and usually the house is full of them."

I planned to think about the plastic bags of water for the remainder of the evening, but other stuff kept getting in the way—Francine's house, for one, which

was really more of a compound: the Francine Institute, with a big modern space for writing, and a separate alcove for the dozens of books she's authored,
and all the products these books have generated, the
dolls and posters and calendars.

Dinner was taken in the backyard beside the
canal. It was a clear night, cold enough to see our
breath, and a fire was burning. Joining us were
Pauline, Francine's ex-husband, and one of their
sons, a twenty-year-old named Dan. Like his mother,
he was blond, with the sort of looks we all might
have were we allowed to construct ourselves from a
kit: perfectly spaced blue eyes, perfect cheekbones, a
perfect mouthful of big white teeth. On top of that
he was really kind and interesting. After dinner we
moved our chairs into a circle around the fire pit and
were served apple cake. Hugh asked a question about
the economy, and Dan explained that the Netherlands has one of the lowest unemployment rates in
Europe. "As long as you get a master's degree you're
pretty much guaranteed a job." He himself was in his
second year of college, majoring in saving the Earth.
"That's not the actual name of the program, but it's
pretty much what it amounts to," he told us.

I asked what sort of things he was learning, and
he brought up a biology class he'd sat through
earlier that week. "We were talking about aging
and how the average life expectancy keeps creeping
upward. It used to be that people died in their
midthirties, but now look at us! And it's all changing so quickly." Dan said that the first person
who'll reach the age of two hundred has already

been born. "It's anyone's guess who it is, but he or she is definitely here."

It could have been the authority in his voice, or maybe the firelight reflected in his eyes, but for whatever reason, this sounded to me like a prophecy. I swallowed the last of my cake and leaned forward to ask a question. "At the age of a hundred sixty, will this person be like, 'You know what? I'm starting to feel a little tired,' or will he be curled into a ball, puddled in drool and Botox?"

"We don't know," Dan said.

I stared into the flames and got a sickening feeling that the person we were talking about would turn out to be my father. And that I would be the one left to care for him. *Think of the plastic bags of water hanging in the doorway,* I told myself, but try as I might, I couldn't get it out of my mind, not then, shivering beside the dark canal, and not later, on our way back to Amsterdam. The taxi meter clicked ever upward, and I saw the figures as ages rather than sums, thinking, *Sixty-six, that's like being in your twenties. Sixty-seven, that's still nothing. When I'm sixty-seven my father will be a mere one hundred years old.*

That would leave him a whole other century to call at odd hours and ask if I'd gotten a colonoscopy. This is a campaign he started in 1978, the first time he had one. "It was horrible," he reported. "The doctor made me take my pants off and strapped me into a kind of bottomless chair—tethered me like a hostage. Then he tipped it forward and stuck, no kidding, a three-foot metal rod up my ass! Can you imagine? There

I was, begging for mercy. Turned practically upside down, sweat dripping off my nose, I mean to tell you it was just god-awful, like torture. The single worst experience of my entire life." Then, in the same breath, he added, "I think you should get one."

"But I'm only twenty-two years old!"

"It's never too early," he told me. "Go on. I'll pay for it myself."

I said to my sister Lisa, "It's like he thinks I'll enjoy it."

I'd heard the procedure was easier now than it was in the late '70s. Rather than being strapped into a chair, you lie on your side, doped to the gills, while a slender tentacle no thicker than packing twine meanders the empty corridors of your colon. "It couldn't be simpler," a doctor promised me. "We knock you out, and you wake up remembering nothing."

"Nothing about you doing God knows what inside my asshole?" I said. "I'm sorry, but that doesn't sound very reassuring to me."

"You're a ticking time bomb," my father said. "Mark my words, you wait much longer and you're going to regret it."

When I hit fifty he doubled his efforts. He doubled them again the following year, and then it was basically all he ever talked about. I had oral surgery in the summer of 2010 and had just returned from the periodontist, my mouth still numb and leaking blood onto my chin, when the phone rang. "Seeing as that's done, I want you to get a colonoscopy," my father said.

I took him with me to a college in New York where I was to give the commencement address, and just before I went onstage he tapped me on the shoulder. "I want you to think about getting a colonoscopy."

He worked it into every conversation we had. The one after I returned from Amsterdam, for instance, when I called to ask what he wanted for Christmas. "I want for you to get a goddamn colonoscopy."

"You want your gift to be someone sticking a foreign object up my ass?"

"You're damn right I do." He continued to hammer at it until, exhausted, I told him I couldn't talk anymore. We hung up, and two minutes later he called again.

"Or an iPhone."

When I think of it, he's actually not a bad candidate for two hundred. Here he is, eighty-nine years old, and he's never once spent a night in the hospital. Four times a week he attends a spinning class at the Y, this in addition to a great deal of walking and dragging things around. His memory is excellent. He does all his own shopping and cooking and has never once called any of us by the wrong name. The secret, he tells me, is to eat seven gin-soaked raisins a day.

"Blond or dark?" I asked.

"Doesn't matter."

"Could I possibly cut out the gin part? Marinate them in, I don't know, coffee or something."

"Do you want to live or don't you?" he asked.

When I told my father about Dan's prophecy, he said, "Aw, baloney. A twenty-year-old kid in Holland, what does he know?"

"He learned it in school."

"No, he didn't," my father said. "The guy was just pulling your leg." He had a similar opinion of the plastic bags hanging in Francine's doorway. "It's just a load of BS."

"As opposed to seven gin-soaked raisins keeping you alive until you're eighty-nine?"

"Hey," he said, "those raisins work!"

If not them, something was doing the trick. He harassed me with the energy of a man half his age until finally, six months after our trip to Amsterdam, I cracked. I was in the United States at the time, in the midst of a thirty-day, thirty-city tour. Once it was over, I planned on visiting my family, and, figuring I'd just be sitting around anyway, I called a North Carolina endoscopy center and made an appointment. The place I chose was not in Raleigh— my father would have insisted on watching—but in Winston-Salem, where Lisa lives.

Booking the procedure two weeks in advance left me plenty of time to collect stories, both good and bad. The part maligned by just about everyone was the preparation. In order for your colon to be properly studied, it has to be empty. To achieve this, you are prescribed a horrific combination of laxatives and stool softeners that essentially chains you to the toilet for a period of twelve to eighteen hours. Some of the people I spoke with had remained conscious during their colonoscopies and had even joined their doctors in watching the footage live on the monitor. These tended to be the same types who did their own taxes and read *Consumer Reports* before buying a dehumidifier or toaster oven. They were, in effect, the types I am not.

As long as somebody knocked me out, I felt that I'd be okay. Then I met a woman who took my fragile peace of mind and shattered it. "The camera up the bottom part was not so bad," she reported. "I was out cold while all that happened, but then I was wheeled into what was called 'the farting room' and told I couldn't leave until I had passed enough gas to satisfy them."

"No!" I said.

"They inflate your colon with air, and you absolutely have to get it out before going home," she told me. "I had a nurse literally pressing on my stomach like she was kneading dough."

"And you had to do that... *in front of people?*"

She closed her eyes and nodded.

"I can't," I told her.

"But you'll have to!"

"No, seriously. I can't."

"I didn't have a farting room," Lisa said when I repeated the woman's story. "At least it wasn't written on the door. And you might think it's crazy, but I loved my colonoscopy." Without my sister's enthusiasm I might have canceled my appointment. As it was, she could not have been more helpful or encouraging. The day before my procedure, she gave me my laxatives and poured my first glass of Gatorade mixed with stool softener. I drank the required thirty-two ounces, I suffered the effects, and the next morning I forced down another bottle. I'd thought that going without solid food for a total of twenty-four hours would leave me peckish and cranky, but I felt no hungrier than usual when, at the appointed time, we headed to the endoscopy center.

At the front desk I checked in and was told that for the rest of the day I would not be able to write checks or make any legal decisions. "Is that okay?" asked the receptionist. She was cheerful and sweet-smelling, and as I picked up her pen to sign my release forms, I noticed the paw prints tattooed on her chest. It looked like she'd been stepped on, or perhaps hugged, by a bobcat with muddy feet.

"Those are darling," Lisa said, and the woman, whose name was Vette, thanked her. Behind us in the waiting room were a half dozen people. All were a good deal older than me, and most were watching television. It wasn't tuned to the news but rather to a loop of brief medical infomercials. "Could you be suffering from an overactive bladder?" the narrator of one of them wondered. Next we were asked to consider irritable bowel syndrome.

"Oh no," Lisa whispered, wincing at the TV. I thought I'd get to sit with her for a while, and maybe learn something new about incontinence, but moments after signing my last form I was led into the back of the building and into the room where my procedure would take place. In its center was a tall hospital bed, and running along one wall was a high shelf loaded with supplies. There might have been a dozen things on it, but what caught my eyes and precluded them from advancing was the K-Y Jelly, which was stored in a tub the size of a bongo drum.

"Would you like me to outline what will be happening to you?" a technician named Dawn asked.

I told her I'd rather not know the details, and she left me alone to undress and step into a backless gown. When that was done, she arranged me upon the tall bed and introduced me to the anesthesiologist, who held an oxygen tube in her hand and asked if I was allergic to latex.

I answered no, wondering, *Am I?* She affixed the tube to my nose and was just inserting an IV into my arm when the gastroenterologist came in. Without quite noticing it, I seem to have reached an age when my doctors are younger than I am. This fellow looked to be in his late thirties. "Holmes" was how he introduced himself—just his last name, with no title. We shook, and a moment later the anesthesiologist connected a syringe full of cream-colored liquid to my IV.

"Now I'm going to ask you to go to your happy place," she said. The back of my gown fell open, and I felt the cool air on my exposed rear end.

"My what?"

"Your happy place," she repeated. "It's different for each person. The man I anesthetized before you, for instance, went to the Augusta golf course, and when he woke up he was winning the Masters."

At first I thought my happy place would be a stage. I was walking from the wings to the podium, excited, like always, by all the attention I would soon be getting, when I changed my mind and revisited the house I grew up in. It was any night in the early 1970s and my sisters and I were sitting around the dining room table, trying to make our mother laugh. I could just see her, head cocked to one side, lighting a cigarette off a candle, when I jumped to a cottage my family rented one summer on the coast of North Carolina, and then to a September afternoon in Normandy. The anesthesiologist emptied her syringe into my IV, and just as I said, "No, wait, I haven't decided yet," or just as I thought I said it, I slipped away into a velvety nothingness.

When I awoke some time later, I was in a different location. Curtains surrounded me on four sides, and through a part in one of them I could see a woman folding papers and putting them into envelopes. I asked her, dreamily, if we had met, and when she told me that we had not, I gave her a little finger wave, the type a leprechaun might offer a pixie who was floating by on a maple leaf. "Well, hi there," I whispered.

Never had I experienced such an all-encompassing sense of well-being. Everything was soft-edged and lovely. Everyone was magnificent. Perhaps if I still drank and took drugs I might not have felt the effects so strongly, but except for some Dilaudid I'd been given for a kidney stone back in 2009, I had been cruelly sober for thirteen years.

"Well, that's propofol for you," Dr. Holmes would later say. "It's what Michael Jackson was injecting himself with when he died."

And who can blame him? I'd give anything to sleep so soundly, and to wake each morning on a cloud of such fuzzy love.

"I'm going to need for you to pass some gas," said the woman putting papers into envelopes. She spoke as if she were a teacher, and I was a second-grade student. "Do you think you can do that for me?"

"For you, anything." And as I did as I was instructed, I realized it was no different than playing a wind instrument. There were other musicians behind other curtains, and I swore I could hear them chiming in, the group of us forming God's own horn section. I'm not sure how long I lay there, blissed-out and farting. Three minutes? Five? Ten? Then I was instructed to get dressed, and someone led me into a room with a newspaper and a Bible in it. There I was reunited with Lisa, who said joyfully, "Didn't I tell you?"

"Oh, you did," I sighed. "I just didn't allow myself to believe it. The next time, we should have these done together. Wouldn't that just be fantastic?"

I was looking at her, beaming, love radiating from my body like heat from a lightbulb, when Dr. Holmes entered and told me it had all gone beautifully. "Congratulations," he said. "You have the colon of a twenty-five-year-old."

I'll fall for anything, apparently. "Really! A twenty-five-year-old!"

"Actually I'm just kidding," he said. "All healthy colons look more or less alike." He gave me some pictures of what the camera had captured, but I couldn't make sense of them—not then, as I bobbed balloonlike off the walls of the tiny room, or later, at

Lisa's house, after the drug had worn off and I was myself again.

I was just getting ready to go for a walk when my father called.

"So?" he asked. "What's your verdict? Was it as bad as you'd thought it would be?"

I wanted to thank him for all the years of pestering me, to concede that he'd had my best interests at heart, but instead, unable to stop myself, I said, "Dad, they found something. And Dad...Daddy...I have cancer."

It's horrible, I know, but I'd somehow been waiting all my life to say those words. During fits of self-pity I had practiced them like lines in a play, never thinking of the person I'd be delivering them to but only of myself, and of how tragic I would sound. The "Daddy" bit surprised me, though, so much so that tears sprang forth and clouded my vision. This made it all the harder to see Lisa, who was listening to me from the other end of the sofa and mouthing what could have been any number of things but was probably, emphatically, *You will go to hell for this.*

"The important thing is not to give in to defeat," my father said. He sounded so strong, so completely his younger, omnipotent self, that I hated to tell him I was kidding. "You've got to fight," he said. "I know that you're scared, but I'm telling you, son, together we can lick this."

Eventually I would set him straight, but until then, at least for another few seconds, I wanted to stay in this happy place. So loved and protected. So fulfilled.

Dog Days

Pepper, Spot, and Leopold
were sent by God, so I've been told,
in hopes we might all comprehend
that every dog is man's best friend.

Hail hyperactive Myrtle,
owned by folks who are infertile.
Her owners boast as she runs wild,
"She's not a spaniel, she's our child!"

Hercules, a Pekingese,
was taken in and dipped for fleas.
Insecticide got in his eyes.
Now he'll be blind until he dies.

Rags, the Shatwells' Irish setter,
doubles as a paper shredder.
His lunch was bills and last year's taxes,
followed by a dozen faxes.

Petunia May they say was struck
chasing down a garbage truck.
A former purebred Boston terrier,
her family's wond'ring where to bury her.

Most every ev'ning Goldilocks
snacks from Kitty's litter box.
Then on command she gives her missus
lots of little doggy kisses.

The Deavers' errant pit bull, Cass,
bit the postman on the ass.
Her lower teeth destroyed his sphincter.
Now his walk's a bit distincter.

Bitches loved the pug Orestes
till the vet snipped off his testes.
Left with only anal glands,
he's now reduced to shaking hands.

Dachshund Skip from Winnipeg
loves to hump his master's leg.
Every time he gets it up, he
stains Bill's calves with unborn puppy.

A naughty Saint Bernard named Don
finds Polly's Kotex in the john.
He holds the blood steak in his jaws
and mourns her coming menopause.

A summer day and shar-pei Boris
sits inside a parked Ford Taurus.

He yaps until his throat is sore,
then pants awhile and yaps some more.

An average day and poor Raquel's
being shot with cancer cells.
Among her friends she likes to crab
that she's a pointer, not a Lab.

Each night old Bowser licks his balls,
then falls asleep till nature calls.
He poops a stool, then, though it's heinous,
bends back down and licks his anus.

About the Author

David Sedaris is the author of the books *Squirrel Seeks Chipmunk*, *When You Are Engulfed in Flames*, *Dress Your Family in Corduroy and Denim*, *Me Talk Pretty One Day*, *Holidays on Ice*, *Naked*, and *Barrel Fever*. He is a regular contributor to *The New Yorker* and BBC Radio 4. He lives in England.